Praise for *The Jury Crisis*

"This book is a gift to the serious trial lawyer. It is easy to read this clear-eyed prose that imparts important, documented information about how juries decide. I am recommending it as required reading for my colleagues, whether they be experienced or novice trial lawyers."

—**Chilton Davis Varner,** King and Spalding,
Former President of American College of Trial Lawyers

"*The Jury Crisis* clearly and concisely describes the various procedures used in the U.S. to resolve legal disputes in the U.S.—jury trials, judge trials, rulings by judges without trial, arbitrations, mediations, settlements. Sherrod uses his training and experience as a psychologist and jury researcher, supported by a broad array of empirical studies performed by himself and other scientists and legal experts, to show how and why juries and judges decide cases as they actually do, rather than how they are commonly thought to decide them. Most importantly, he presents powerful arguments for preserving jury trials by making much-needed improvements in the way trials are conducted."

—**Malcolm E. Wheeler,** Founding Partner/
Counsel Emeritus, Wheeler Trigg O'Donnnell LLP

"Over his distinguished career in jury research, Drury Sherrod has advised hundreds of lawyers on how best to shape and present their case arguments. In this book, he educates the reader about the challenges jury trials face today and offers concrete recommendations about saving this critical institution. After years of counselling lawyers on storytelling, Sherrod demonstrates his own special storytelling for the reader."

—**Michael L. O'Donnell,**
Chairman of Wheeler Trigg O'Donnell

The Jury Crisis

The Jury Crisis

What's Wrong with Jury Trials and How We Can Save Them

Drury R. Sherrod

ROWMAN & LITTLEFIELD
Lanham • Boulder • New York • London

Published by Rowman & Littlefield
An imprint of The Rowman & Littlefield Publishing Group, Inc.
4501 Forbes Boulevard, Suite 200, Lanham, Maryland 20706
www.rowman.com

6 Tinworth Street, London SE11 5AL, United Kingdom

British Library Cataloguing in Publication Information Available

Library of Congress Cataloging-in-Publication Data

Names: Sherrod, Drury R., author.
Title: The jury crisis : what's wrong with jury trials and how we can save them / Drury R. Sherrod.
Description: Lanham, Md. : Rowman & Littlefield, 2019. | Includes bibliographical references.
Identifiers: LCCN 2018027686 (print) | LCCN 2018027865 (ebook) |
    ISBN 9781538109540 (electronic) | ISBN 9781538109533 (cloth : alk. paper)
Subjects: LCSH: Jury—United States.
Classification: LCC KF9680 (ebook) | LCC KF9680 .S54 2019 (print) |
    DDC 347.73/752—dc23
LC record available at https://lccn.loc.gov/2018027686

∞™ The paper used in this publication meets the minimum requirements of American National Standard for Information Sciences—Permanence of Paper for Printed Library Materials, ANSI/NISO Z39.48-1992.

Printed in the United States of America

For Arden
And for Bert,
Who touch me deeply
Everyday

Contents

x ~ Contents

Acknowledgments

Several people helped shape the evolution of this book. My partner, Arden Reed, inspired, supported, and contributed to early versions of all the chapters, helping to make the thinking sharper and the writing more felicitous. Alicia Miller encouraged the project from day 1. Paul Hultin helped launch and frame the project by sponsoring a legal conference that led to the writing. Rena Fraden reviewed the manuscript with a reader's eye and a professor's questions. My former student Elizabeth Steele filtered the text through a lawyer's attention to detail. My friend Mickey Klein, who knows something about litigating, read and commented on an early version. Kevin Dettmar suggested useful changes in final editing. My business partner Larry Mattson provided a context for analyzing jury trials and jurors. Eric Gober and Sean Overland performed important data analyses. And countless people who regaled me with stories about their jury experience convinced me that juries matter and jury trials are fundamental to democracy.

Introduction
What's Wrong with Juries?

Flanked by flags, robed in black, peering down from the bench, a judge sternly instructs jurors on what they must do to return a verdict: "Keep an open mind until you have heard all the evidence. Consider only what has been presented in court. Weigh the facts carefully. Deliberate together until you have reached a unanimous verdict." But jurors seldom obey a judge's instructions. They can't help it. The human brain doesn't function the way the court says it should, and lawyers and judges don't make the jurors' job any easier. As a result, juries have gotten a bad reputation. People cringe when they receive a jury summons. Jurors are seen as incompetent and unpredictable, and jury trials, a waste of money and time. So few disputes come before a jury today that the American jury trial is on the verge of extinction.

A recent white-collar criminal case in New York offers a classic example of almost everything that can go wrong in a jury trial.[1] The once-prominent law firm Dewey & LeBoeuf suffered a financial crisis and collapsed. Suspicious that several partners had manipulated the firm's financial records, the Manhattan district attorney charged three former Dewey executives with fraud. The trial went on for four-and-a-half months. More than forty witnesses were called. The jury listened to hours of testimony about complex accounting law and saw scores of e-mails, a flood of documents, piles of records, and stacks of ledger pages. At the end of the trial, the jury of seven women and five men was instructed to reach a verdict on each of more than 150 separate charges against the three defendants. After an extraordinary twenty-one days of deliberations and finding the defendants not guilty on several dozen minor charges, the jury informed the judge that it was "hopelessly deadlocked" on the remaining ninety-three charges. The judge was forced to declare a mistrial.

When several jurors were interviewed after the trial, they painted a picture of near-total confusion and floundering in the jury room. One woman reported that many of her fellow jurors were "uncertain as to what our role as jurors was." Some people didn't understand what the task of "deliberation" required, so the foreperson sent the judge a note asking for an explanation. Others were uncertain how to proceed in order to find guilt "beyond a reasonable doubt." One juror said several of her colleagues "refused to budge or explain their positions, while others seemed to change their minds constantly, sometimes on what seemed little more than a whim." "Some jurors closed their eyes and refused to listen when other jurors spoke," a female juror reported. "And there was a great deal of hostility, both overt and covert." As a result, four of the twelve jurors dug in their heels and refused to acquit the three executives. The jury hung.

The same thing happened in the first of two high-profile jury trials when one of America's best-known entertainers, comedian Bill Cosby, was sued for "aggravated indecent assault" after he allegedly drugged and raped a woman in his home in 2004. If convicted, Mr. Cosby could have been punished with up to ten years in prison. After six days of testimony from the woman who accused Mr. Cosby, along with experts' opinions on sexual assault and the effects of mind-numbing drugs, the trial went to a jury. The jury of six white men, four white women, one black man, and one black woman then deliberated for fifty-two hours, as much as twelve hours a day, longer than it took to present each side's evidence. On the sixth day of deliberations, the jury foreman sent the judge a note, saying the jury was hopelessly deadlocked. The judge declared a mistrial.[2]

In the days after the mistrial, reporters repeatedly tried to contact the jurors to ask what had happened in the jury room. After a week of silence, two jurors cracked under the pressure and granted interviews. "The deliberation room was so tiny and cramped," these jurors said. "There was no room to pace." "Many people were in tears," and at several points, bailiffs entered the room because they believed "fights were breaking out." After thirty long hours of deliberations, the jury was deadlocked, and "no one budged" for the remaining twenty-two hours. One reason for the deadlock, according to both jurors whom reporters contacted, was that the language of the charges was confusing:

> They were legally written with a lot of different words than what was said in the courtroom . . . like "reckless," and "unconscious" and "severely impaired" and "unreasonable doubt," one juror said. We spent a lot of time trying to figure out these words that were in the charge. . . . We never heard those

words, and that's where the problem was. "Reckless" was one word we spent a whole day trying to figure out. You couldn't convict him on the wording of the charges. And that's where we argued back and forth. What meant one thing to one person [meant] something [else] to another.[3]

Because of this confusion, the jury sent several notes to the judge, asking such questions as "What is reasonable doubt?" and "Please define 'without her knowledge.'" Unfortunately, none of the questions was answered by the judge in a way that changed the jurors' minds.

While the Dewey & LeBoeuf trial was unusually long and complex and the charges in the Cosby trial were confusing, jurors' difficulty understanding the evidence and reaching a verdict in both of these trials is not unusual. Even in much shorter, simpler trials, jurors misunderstand evidence, ignore the judge's instructions, and arrive at seemingly arbitrary verdicts. Such problems raise questions about the future of trial by jury, which this book addresses.

Can Juries Be Improved?

The Sixth Amendment to the United States Constitution guarantees "in all criminal proceedings a speedy and public trial, by an impartial jury." The Seventh Amendment extends this right to "suits at common law," or noncriminal disputes, where individuals and corporations sue each other. The Seventh Amendment notably declares that "no fact tried by a jury, shall be otherwise reexamined in any Court of the United States." Hidden within the apparent simplicity of just a few words in these two amendments are the questions at the heart of this book. Can a jury be impartial in today's United States? What does it mean to try a fact, when the facts are sometimes barely knowable and the triers are inherently biased? How can an impartial jury try facts conclusively, when jurors fail to understand the law and are unable to follow complex evidence presented by countless witnesses over days, weeks, or months? If no satisfactory answers exist for these questions, then should trial by jury be abandoned? Should the whole process of dispensing justice be handed over to "experts," that is, judges, mediators, and arbitrators, who might be more skilled at finding right from wrong?

As a PhD social psychologist and a longtime partner in one of America's leading jury research firms, I bring two perspectives to the task of explaining, and perhaps resolving, the dilemmas of trial by jury. One perspective is rooted in the empirical research on jury decision making. This research focuses on how a juror's brain jumps to conclusions, favors "hunches" over rational analysis, and resorts to mental shortcuts in reaching (or failing to reach) a verdict. It explains how a juror's life experience influences how a juror sees the evidence in a case. And it explores how jurors behave during deliberations, where groupthink often leads to "quick and dirty" verdicts, or when jurors simply dig in their heels and refuse to talk to other jurors.

The other perspective reflects thirty years of practical experience selecting jurors, attending trials, interviewing jurors when trials conclude, running mock trials (miniversions of real trials, with mock jurors recruited to match a local jury panel), observing mock-trial deliberations, developing persuasive trial strategies, and writing opening statements for civil trials in courtrooms across America. Combining the psychological perspective with practical experience in real and mock trials provides me with an unusually broad yet intimate perspective on how juries work and how they can work better. My goal in this book is to raise and answer questions that can help determine the future of trial by jury.

Prominent law professor Adam Benforado recently charged that "our legal system is based on an inaccurate model of human behavior." So inaccurate is this model, he says, that today's jury trials will seem as "laughable" to future generations as a medieval "trial by ordeal" sounds to us today. To correct these "fundamental flaws," he concludes, "our justice system must be reconstructed upon scientific fact."[4]

Among the specific questions and science-based answers I consider in this book are the following: How capable are jurors of carrying out their essential duty of fact finding and reaching a verdict? At what point in a trial do jurors typically make up their minds? Do they wait, as the judge instructs them, until they have heard all the evidence? Or might they leap to an intuitive conclusion when a trial is barely underway? Do jurors rely strictly on the evidence presented in court? Or might they fabricate, embellish, and distort evidence based on their own personal experiences? Might they ignore evidence and witnesses they can't understand?

Do jurors from different backgrounds view the same evidence so differently that they actually "see" different evidence? How strongly do jurors' built-in biases influence their views of the evidence? Can a juror's verdict be predicted in advance, the way a voter's ballot choice can be predicted? If we know a juror's gender, ethnicity, life experiences, and attitudes about the type of issues raised in a trial, then do we already know the juror's likely verdict? If jurors' verdicts are indeed predictable, can a trial be won during jury selection, before any evidence is presented? Is winning simply a matter of striking, or excluding, the "wrong" jurors and keeping the "right" jurors, as each side defines them? Does the evidence even matter?

Beyond the biases that jurors themselves may bring into the courtroom, the presentation of trial evidence is often confusing to people unfamiliar with trial procedure. Evidence is generally presented in bits and pieces through examination and cross-examination of witnesses. Witnesses may appear in no logical order. The result is a fragmentary scattershot of contradictory statements that jurors must try to assemble into a meaningful sequence. Can evidence be presented differently, in a way that better matches the human brain's own processes? If, as later chapters show, the brain evolved to construct stories and seek information that supports familiar stories, then is it realistic to expect jurors to refrain from storytelling and keep an open mind until they have rationally analyzed hundreds or thousands of bits of evidence over weeks and months of a trial? Instead, should trial evidence be presented more like a story, so jurors can more easily track the evidence and assemble it into a pattern?

Another set of problems arises when jurors retire to deliberate. When the door to the jury room is closed and jurors sit face to face around a table to decide a verdict, do they review all of the evidence and reason together before making a decision, as the judge instructs? Or do they begin by stating their private feelings and then seek allies for their causes? Are unanimous verdicts always truly unanimous, or do some jurors simply cave and comply with the majority in order to go home? Do jurors' genders, ethnicities, and class differences lead to such divergent appraisals of the facts that a unanimous, or near-unanimous, verdict is often impossible?

Finally, it is legitimate to ask if trial by jury is still a reasonable way of resolving disputes a thousand years after the concept emerged in rural English villages in a far different world than our own. Are the issues in many of today's trials more complex than nonexperts can comprehend? Can a jury of one's peers be assembled in a society so multicultural that even the definition of peer is questionable? If we abandon trial by jury, then are there alternative ways to resolve disputes that work any better than a jury, such as relying on judges, mediators, or arbitrators? Or do judges and other legal experts bring their own biases to the table?

Taken together, the answers to these questions open the closed door of the jury room and reveal how and why jurors reach the verdicts they reach. By the end of this book, you should be able to say whether America's trust in trial by jury is truly justified or woefully misplaced. The conclusions will be useful for citizen jurors, for lawyers who try cases before jurors, and for policy makers who are concerned about a more just United States.

Chapter Preview

Chapter 1 unpacks the juror's role as a trier of fact. It reviews several actual cases where the facts are so vague, so open to interpretation, or so unknowable that a juror is forced to construct a story from personal experience in order to imagine what must have happened in a dispute. Hearing about these cases, the reader, too, must wrestle with the dilemma of fact versus story, as the reader searches for a fair verdict.

Chapter 2 reviews the slow evolution of jury trials from "self-informing" medieval jurors to "witness-informed" jurors in the modern era. Regardless of how jurors become informed about the evidence in a case, however, this chapter argues that jury trials historically required and expected jurors to construct stories as a pathway to verdicts. For most of the centuries when some form of trial by jury has existed, the chapter notes, jury trials and jury deliberations were often so brief that many were conducted in a single day, which forced jurors to rely on stories instead of facts.

Chapter 3 explores the story model for jury decision making. This chapter looks at psychological research that shows that jurors intuitively convert evidence into stories. Such research demonstrates that jurors' stories influence their verdicts and that presenting evidence in a narrative format is more persuasive than presenting evidence in an out-of-order, non-narrative, witness-driven format, as many, if not most, attorneys do. The chapter draws on an actual case introduced in chapter 1 as an illustrative example.

Chapter 4 then explains why jurors tell stories when they hear trial evidence. It reviews psychological research demonstrating that the human brain evolved to favor fast, intuitive, narrative-style explanations over slow, rational, analytical explanations. It argues that jurors are unable to switch from narrative explanations to analytical explanations just because a judge instructs them to.

Chapters 5 through 8 deal with how the story model for jury decision making can be applied in the courtroom. Chapter 5 focuses on jury selection and uses the controversial Trayvon Martin murder trial as an example of how jurors' experiences and attitudes can predict the stories they will likely construct about the evidence in a criminal trial. The chapter also shows how jurors' likely stories can be determined during jury selection and how attorneys can decide which jurors to strike and which to keep on a jury.

Chapter 6 moves from criminal to civil trials. Drawing on mock trials from my thirty years as a jury consultant, this chapter discusses specific attitudes and life experiences that lead jurors to construct stories favoring plaintiffs or defendants in product liability lawsuits, where hundreds of millions of dollars may be at stake. It also contrasts the characteristics of jurors who are likely to award high damages versus low damages and identifies which jurors are likely to award punitive damages.

Chapter 7 opens a rare window onto how juries reach a verdict. Deliberations are the least known and least understood part of a trial because jury deliberations are never observed nor transcribed. Chapter 7 shows how juries are uniquely subject to the pressures and stresses of groupthink. The chapter argues that these pressures can undermine the ideal of deliberations and lead jurors in the majority to ignore the views of jurors in the minority in a rush to judgment.

Chapter 8 reinforces the arguments in chapter 7 by drawing on numerous highly revealing post-trial juror interviews I and my firm have conducted, which show how groupthink influences deliberations in real trials. Jurors often ignore the judge's instructions, immediately announce their individual story-based verdicts before any deliberations begin, seek allies among other jurors who tell similar stories, use evidence strategically to bolster their stories, ignore evidence inconsistent with their stories, liberally augment their stories with details from personal experience, and sometimes abruptly change their minds in order to go home.

After focusing on the many ways that jurors' verdicts are almost unavoidably influenced by storytelling, the book turns in chapter 9 to alternatives to jurors—namely, judges. Are judges any less resistant to storytelling than jurors? Drawing on the results of mock bench trials conducted by my firm and involving judges instead of jurors, chapter 9 shows how judges can interpret the same facts differently, disagree among themselves, reach widely different verdicts on the same cases, and be just as biased as jurors. The chapter also outlines the many ways in which judges' biases can influence their rulings during jury trials.

Chapter 10 continues the focus on judges as an alternative to jurors. But this chapter examines recent psychological research that documents the extent of judges' biased storytelling at all levels of the US court system. This chapter concludes that judges' decisions are affected both by their political philosophies and by the opinions of fellow judges—much as jurors are influenced by groupthink.

Having established that judges are not a bias-free alternative to juries and should not be substituted for juries, chapter 11 examines the disturbing phenomenon of the "vanishing jury." Given the dissatisfaction with jury verdicts because of their length, cost, and unpredictability, this chapter documents how trial by jury is becoming extinct in America. It shows how juries are being replaced by arbitrators, mediators, and "private" judges, who not only bring their own biases to a case but also whose biases are not subject to the moderating influence of a group of six to twelve ordinary citizens.

Chapter 12 then asks what will be lost if juries vanish. Will verdicts be any fairer when rendered by "experts"? Would democracy suffer from the demise of the jury? What will happen if a fundamental check on the power of the state disappears?

Finally, chapter 13 reviews numerous ways that trial by jury can be reformed. The book concludes with specific research-based recommendations about what courts, judges, attorneys, and jurors themselves can do to improve and retain trial by jury.

⚖

CHAPTER ONE

Triers of Fact

A few years ago, in a small southern town, a young man picked up his girl-friend for her 7:30 dinner break from the late shift at Walmart. The couple drove to a nearby fast-food restaurant, ordered some fried chicken, and sat down at a booth. Minutes later, a young, off-duty, male employee of the restaurant dropped by to check his work schedule for the following day. Not long after this man arrived, a female employee of the restaurant took her evening break. The off-duty male employee and the female employee on her break sat down in a booth to talk. A few minutes later, they decided to move to a different booth. The new booth they chose happened to back up to the booth where the woman from Walmart was seated, across the table from her boyfriend. As the off-duty male employee dropped his backpack onto the seat of the booth, a handgun in the pack somehow fired. The bullet shot into the back of the booth, came out the other side, and penetrated the spine of the young woman who was having dinner with her boyfriend. The gunshot left the woman permanently paralyzed from the waist down.

Once an active runner, the woman—who happened to be at the wrong place at the wrong time—is now confined to a wheelchair for the rest of her life. She cannot move her body below the waist. She experiences frequent pain. Her boyfriend broke up with her because of her condition and because his mobile home where they had been living was not wheelchair accessible. The young woman moved in with her mother, whose cramped apartment barely accommodated the wheelchair. Because of her partial paralysis, the woman lost her job. Since then, she has drifted through a series of jobs that allow her to work as a paraplegic.

Who is responsible for the young woman's plight? The off-duty employee whose gun fired a bullet into the woman's spine spent a year in prison for possessing a weapon under age and for carrying a concealed handgun without a permit. But what was the restaurant's role? The woman who was paralyzed filed a civil lawsuit against the corporation that owns the restaurant. She argued that the restaurant must be held responsible for the conduct of its employees. She asked that a jury hear her case.

The Jury's Job

Let's return for a moment to the Seventh Amendment to the United States Constitution, the amendment that deals with civil trials, such as the young woman's lawsuit against the restaurant where she was shot. The Seventh Amendment clearly delineates the role of a jury in a civil trial. It reads in its entirety, "In Suits at common law, where the value in controversy shall exceed twenty dollars, the right of trial by jury shall be preserved, and no fact tried by a jury, shall be otherwise re-examined in any Court of the United States, than according to the rules of common law." Significantly, the Seventh Amendment of the United States Constitution assigns jurors the role of "triers of fact." It further states that, when a jury has determined the facts of a case, the facts cannot be reexamined by "any Court of the United States." While a court may reexamine whether a jury applied the relevant law correctly, a court cannot, except in very rare circumstances, reexamine a jury's determination of the facts. The facts stand as the jury sees them.

But what does it mean for a jury to try a fact? According to the *Oxford English Dictionary, to try* means "to ascertain the truth." A *fact* is defined as "something that has really occurred or is actually the case." So a jury's role is to ascertain the truth about what really occurred. This sounds straightforward, but let's now look at four lawsuits, each of which presented jurors with a different challenge about what the "facts" mean. The first is the gunshot injury lawsuit in a restaurant, where a jury had to determine how the gun fired and who could have prevented it. The second is the storied McDonald's coffee case, which asked a jury to decide when hot coffee was too hot to be safe. The third is another case from my jury research experience, where jurors were required to "fill in" missing facts in order to understand how a little girl was choked to death by an automobile's power window. And the fourth involved a jury's assessment of a driver's responsibility for an accident, in which class and privilege seemed to influence jurors' decisions.

Case 1: Deciding Responsibility When the Facts Are Unclear

Imagine you are on the jury deciding whether the corporation that owns and operates the restaurant where the woman was shot in the back should be required to compensate her for her injuries. She requested millions of dollars for her gunshot-induced paralysis, for her suffering, and for her lost future income due to the limited range of jobs that are now available to her. How would you try the facts of this case? Could the restaurant have prevented the accident? *Should* the restaurant have prevented the accident? Or was the whole thing a tragic fluke?

Chances are, you are already leaning in one direction: either finding for the young woman or finding for the corporation. On one hand, you may have decided that the entire episode was a bizarre accident that no one could have predicted and that it would be unfair to hold the restaurant responsible for the young woman's injury. You might have noted that neither the off-duty male employee nor the female employee on her break was under the restaurant's control when the accident occurred. You may ask, "How can the restaurant be held responsible for what happened?"

On the other hand, you may have concluded that the gun would never have been in the restaurant in the first place if the off-duty employee had not been required to confirm his work schedule for the next day by either visiting the restaurant or phoning the manager. Even if he was not on duty at the time of the shooting, he was acting as an employee when he fulfilled his obligation to stop by and confirm his schedule. This makes the restaurant responsible for his actions, you might decide.

The woman on her break originally testified that the off-duty employee showed her his gun during her break, although she subsequently retracted this statement. If the female employee had indeed known about the gun, even if she became aware of the gun while on her break, then you may think it was her duty to alert the manager. After all, the woman was wearing her uniform on the premises, and she admitted under oath that, if a patron had spilled a supersized Coke while she was on break, then she would have recognized the spill as a hazard and cleaned it up. Was not the unlicensed concealed handgun as hazardous as a spilled Coke? Did the woman on her break have a duty to report the gun to her manager because she was an employee of the restaurant? If the woman on break had reported the gun to her manager, then would the manager have ordered the off-duty employee to leave because the restaurant had a policy that off-duty employees could not "loiter" in the restaurant? If the man was indeed loitering and the manager had enforced the no-loitering policy, then you might conclude that the entire episode would have been avoided.

A complicating factor is the question of how the gun got cocked. The particular handgun in this case could only be fired by pulling the trigger or by cocking the hammer and then applying a certain amount of force to the cocked hammer in order to release it. Even though there was no testimony whatsoever about what made the gun fire, chances are that you are already imagining alternative scenarios. Maybe, in an act of heedless bravado, the young man carried a cocked gun in his backpack, and the gun happened to fire when the man dropped his backpack onto the seat of the booth. It is highly unlikely, though, that anyone even remotely familiar with guns would carry a cocked revolver in a backpack in close contact with his body, no matter how heedless the person might be.

Alternatively, you may surmise that the gun was not cocked but that something in the young man's backpack accidentally pulled or pressed against the trigger when the backpack was dropped onto the seat of the booth. But what could have wrapped around the trigger and pulled it with enough force to fire the gun, when the backpack was dropped only a few inches onto the bench? On the other hand, you might propose that a book or a sneaker or something else may have pushed against the gun's hammer with just enough force, first, to pull the hammer back and cock it and, second, to snap the hammer forward and release the bullet. Given the amount of pressure required, though, and the improbable angles of physical contact in a stuffed backpack, neither of these scenarios seems very plausible.

An entirely different scenario was proposed by jurors when the lawsuit was presented in a mock trial. After sitting through a day and a half of arguments and evidence, one very proper older lady said during deliberations, "You know that boy wanted to impress that girl by showing her the gun in his backpack." Another lady immediately added, "That's right. And you know if that girl saw that boy's gun, she'd want to touch it." This is how the two ladies reasoned that the gun had been removed from the backpack, became cocked either accidentally or deliberately by the man or woman, and was then reinserted into the backpack in a cocked position. Under this scenario, when the backpack was dropped on the seat, something pushed against the cocked hammer with enough force to fire the gun.

As you can see from this brief discussion, the "facts" of this lawsuit are virtually unknowable. The relevant state law about an employer's responsibility for an off-duty employee's conduct is ambiguous. Does stopping by a place of employment while an employee is off duty automatically put that employee under the employer's supervision? Was the off-duty employee acting within the "scope and function" of his duty when he stopped by to confirm his hours? Does an employee's becoming aware of an unlicensed, concealed weapon while on break constitute an obligation by that employee to alert her manager to a potential hazard? Is an employee acting within the "scope and function" of her duty while on break? Is an unlicensed, concealed weapon, in fact, a hazard? What if the weapon was thought not to be cocked? And how and when did the gun get cocked? Even if the woman on her break had alerted her manager about a cocked gun, would ejecting the off-duty employee have created a greater hazard than keeping silent about the gun?

What should a trier of fact conclude in this case? The answer may be whatever the trier imagines the facts to be. In other words, a juror's duty "to ascertain the truth about what really occurred" in this case requires the juror to make assumptions, to fill in gaps, to rely on personal experience, to create theories, to interpret the law regarding the "scope and function" of an employee's obligations when off duty, and to reach a verdict based on the juror's individual appraisals. So trying facts may, in fact, amount to constructing a personally satisfying story about what must have happened in an ambiguous situation. Such a story then serves to rationalize a verdict that a juror may reach long before deliberations. And this may often be the best a juror can do.

Case 2: Assessing a Hazard When the Facts Are Known
Even when the facts seem to be clear, a jury's interpretation of the facts can be surprising. Take the infamous McDonald's coffee case. In the twenty-five years since this case was decided by a jury, I have seldom run a mock trial or met with a group of attorneys when someone has not mentioned the McDonald's coffee case as an example of how unpredictable and inexplicable—or even how nutty—a jury can be.

In February 1992, a seventy-nine-year-old Albuquerque woman named Stella Liebeck ordered a $0.49 cup of coffee from the drive-through window of her local McDonald's. Mrs. Liebeck was riding in the passenger's seat of her grandson's Ford Probe, a two-door sports coupe. To give his grandmother time to add cream and sugar to her coffee, the young man pulled the Probe to the side of the parking lot and came to a stop. Mrs. Liebeck placed the Styrofoam cup of coffee on the seat between her knees, opened the cream and sugar packets, and began to peel the cup's plastic lid off the far edge of the cup. As she tugged the lid toward her, the cup tilted and spilled its full serving of hot coffee onto Mrs. Liebeck's lap. Because she was wearing cotton sweatpants, the fabric quickly absorbed the hot liquid and pressed tightly against her skin. The coffee scalded Mrs. Liebeck's thighs, groin, and buttocks. She was immediately taken to the hospital, where it was found that she had suffered third-degree burns on 6 percent of her body. She spent eight days in the hospital and received skin grafts to correct the burns. Her medical bills totaled $10,500. After leaving the hospital, she underwent two more years of medical treatment.

Because of her extensive burns, Mrs. Liebeck hired a lawyer to ask McDonald's to help pay her medical bills and expenses. Her lawyer requested $20,000 from McDonald's to cover Mrs. Liebeck's past and expected future medical care, as well as lost income from being out of work. McDonald's responded with an offer of $800. When McDonald's refused to offer any more money, Mrs. Liebeck's attorney filed a lawsuit against McDonald's. The lawsuit claimed that the McDonald's Corporation was "grossly negligent" because the restaurant served its coffee at a "dangerously high" temperature, which made the coffee "defective."

After the lawsuit was filed, McDonald's refused the plaintiff's settlement offer of $90,000.00. The case went to mediation, and the mediator suggested a much higher amount of $225,000 to settle the case, but McDonald's refused this, too. The case then went to trial, and on the day after the trial ended, the jury found McDonald's 80 percent responsible for Mrs. Liebeck's burns and Mrs. Liebeck herself 20 percent responsible. The jury awarded $200,000 in compensatory damages to cover Ms. Liebeck's expenses.

But the jury did not stop there. It went on to award $2.7 million in punitive damages. The huge award of punitive damages—almost fourteen times the amount of compensatory damages—was so enormous that the case immediately became synonymous with frivolous lawsuits. Although a judge reduced the awards to $160,000 in compensatory damages and $480,000 in punitive damages, McDonald's appealed the verdict. The parties eventually settled out of court for an amount reported to be less than $600,000. However, the McDonald's coffee case still stands in the popular imagination as an example of jury verdicts run amuck.

At this point, you would not be alone if you were thinking, "What a ridiculous verdict!" But there is more to the story. During the trial, the plaintiff showed that McDonald's directed its restaurant operators to serve cups of coffee at 180 to 190 degrees Fahrenheit. Coffee served this hot will stay nicely warm during a long commute, but if it spills on human skin, then it can cause a third-degree burn in two to seven seconds. The plaintiff showed that many restaurants in America, even fast-food chains, served their coffee at much lower temperatures. The plaintiff also revealed that McDonald's had received more than seven hundred complaints of burns from hot coffee, and the company had paid out more than a half-million dollars to settle these claims. While extremely high, the original punitive damage award of $2.7 million dollars was calculated by the jury as merely two days of McDonald's revenues from coffee sales, an amount the jury believed was sufficient to attract McDonald's attention to the perceived risk of serving third-degree-burn-inflicting coffee to people in automobiles, where coffee can easily spill.

What the controversial McDonald's coffee case comes down to is the question of how hot is too hot. The fact that jurors had to try was whether coffee served at more than 180 degrees Fahrenheit was "dangerously hot." What jurors had to weigh was the predictable ease of spilling hot coffee in a car, coupled with the known consequence that coffee spilled at that temperature could inflict third-degree burns in seconds. When such a predictable event and such a known consequence are matched with the image of an elderly woman spilling scalding coffee over her groin, buttocks, and thighs and spending more than a week in the hospital while receiving skin grafts, the jury verdict becomes more understandable and perhaps less outrageous.

Although we have no record of how the McDonald's jury actually reached its verdict, we can gather a few clues. The fact that the twelve-person jury returned a verdict just one day after the trial ended suggests there was apparently little disagreement among the jurors. Perhaps most jurors had already made up their minds when they retired to deliberate over the evidence. It must not have been hard for the jurors to construct a story that superhot coffee, capable of rendering third-degree burns in seconds, is unreasonably hazardous when served in an environment where spills are likely and predictable. And if McDonald's had ignored seven hundred previous complaints, then the company may have seemed fairly callous to the jurors, which apparently justified the punitive damages award.

Case 3: Imagining What Happened When the Facts Are Missing
In a lawsuit filed a few years ago, an automaker was accused by a midwestern family of making a defective power-window switch. The switch looked like a shallow V: If you pressed on one side of the switch, then the window went up; if you pressed on the other side, then it went down. Pressing on the "up" side caused the window to rise with a certain degree of pounds-per-minute force. If a small dog accidentally stepped on the "up" side of the switch while its head was out of the window, then the rising window could elevate the dog's body, the glass pressing against its throat. If the dog's legs were too short to stand on the arm rest, then the dog could hang.

The lawsuit in question involved a two-year-old girl, who stuck her head out of the open window on the front-passenger side of a parked car while her mother sat in the driver's seat. Her mother had left the ignition on, so the radio would play as they sat in the car. But leaving the ignition on also enabled the power-window switch. As the mother rested, the child climbed onto the passenger door's arm rest so she could thrust her head farther outside. Her foot accidentally stepped on the "up" side of the power-window switch. The window silently slid up, elevating the child and trapping her neck between the top of the door frame and the edge of the rising window. The pressure of the window against her throat cut off the little girl's breathing, and she died.

The child's family filed a lawsuit, claiming that the auto manufacturer was at fault for the design of the power-window switch because it shouldn't have been so easy to make the window go up accidentally. In a mock trial, however, the majority of the jurors saw the facts quite differently. The jury heard that the girl's mother and father were from Latin America, that the mother and daughter had been watching the girl's father play in a soccer match, and that the mother pulled the car off the road to rest on the way home from the game. Jurors also heard that, when the mother saw what had happened to her daughter, she tried to press the "down" side of the switch to lower the window and free the little girl. The window failed to go down, however, because the power to the switch had automatically turned off in order to prevent the motor from burning out when the rising window encountered an obstacle. Finally, the jurors heard that the power was designed not to turn off for at least sixty seconds after an obstacle interfered with the rising window. This fact suggested that a minute or more must have passed between the time the girl became trapped and the time the mother tried to rescue her.

Hearing these facts, the majority of the mock jurors decided that the little girl's mother had been drinking "because that's what Latin Americans do at soccer games," a juror said. This "fact," for which no evidence was presented, helped persuade a majority of jurors that the mother had passed out as she rested in the parked car. This inference explained why the mother failed to respond for at least a minute to the choking and crying sounds that, the jury believed, the girl must have made as the rising window pressed against her throat. Another mock juror added, "I've been to Latin America. They don't care much about human life. They sell babies on the street there." No one challenged this juror's statement. As a result of these presumed facts, a majority of the mock jurors concluded that the manufacturer was not at fault because the girl's mother could have prevented her daughter's death had the mother not fallen asleep from drinking too much alcohol. The manufacturer was acquitted.

The jury's verdict in this mock trial clearly involves biases about the beverage preferences of Latin American soccer moms and about the alleged value of babies in Latin America. At the same time, the verdict reveals the power of a jury's made-up stories to influence their assignment of responsibility for a child's death and their appraisal of the alleged hazards of a power-window switch.

Interestingly, in the years since this lawsuit was filed, virtually all power-window switches have been redesigned. Chances are, in your own car, you cannot press down on one side of the switch to make the window go up. You probably have to pull up on one end of the switch to make the window rise. This "pull-up" design ensures that neither dogs nor children can accidentally stand on the window switch and hang themselves as the window rises.

Case 4: Interpreting the Facts from a Personal Perspective

Another mock trial from a few years ago demonstrates how the facts of a case may be appraised differently because of a juror's class and life experiences. This lawsuit involved a dispute between a wealthy family and the manufacturer of a high-end sports utility vehicle.

As Hurricane Katrina approached the US mainland, a Gulf Coast family worried about potential damage to their beach house. The father decided to send his wife and two teenaged daughters to safety, while he attempted to protect his property from the "storm of the century." The women drove to Disney World in Florida, where they stayed until the storm had passed. As the wife was driving their daughters home, she telephoned her husband on her cell phone to hear about the damage to their beach house. During this conversation, the sports utility vehicle somehow veered off the highway, crossed the left shoulder, and went onto the grassy median at a fairly high speed, according to the tire tracks. To get back onto the highway, the wife turned the steering wheel sharply to the right. This caused the vehicle to slide diagonally down the highway, until it eventually flipped over and rolled several times at high speed. During one of the rolls, the roof over the driver's seat crushed in with enough force to break the women's spine and leave her a quadriplegic. The two daughters received only minor injuries.

The family sued the auto manufacturer, claiming that the vehicle was unstable and the roof was weak. While some jurors were persuaded by the family's claims, a majority of jurors in the mock trial decided in favor of the manufacturer. Some thought the driver must have been distracted during her cell phone call. Another frankly admitted that she had a hard time sympathizing with the family's plight. As this juror stated, "We were in the middle of a hurricane. Thousands of people were losing their homes. And this lady was off shaking hands with Mickey Mouse. I have no sympathy."

Can Jurors Be Trusted to Try the Facts?

These four cases may have left you thinking that justice is like a muddy bog. Jurors stumble through the tangled evidence as they try to "ascertain the truth about what really occurred." You might ask in dismay, "Are many cases this open to constructing stories, filling in gaps, imagining scenarios, and interpreting events based on personal experience?" The simple answer is yes. And that's exactly why the jury system matters. Everyday people, in their wisdom, determine facts that are otherwise unknowable.

Most cases that reach a jury in America feature highly disputed facts. When a lawsuit offers reasonably clear facts, then it is likely to be resolved without ever reaching a jury. For example, in a process called summary judgment, one of the litigants in a lawsuit will ask a judge to review the facts and the law governing a case and render a judgment before the case goes to trial. If the judge makes a ruling and the ruling is not appealed by either litigant, then the judgment stands, and the case is closed. Many other lawsuits are resolved through arbitration, when a professional arbitrator hears each side's evidence and delivers a binding decision. Still others conclude after mediation, when an expert mediator reviews the evidence and proposes a solution that both sides agree to accept. Other cases are simply settled by the opposing sides without ever passing before a judge, an arbitrator, a mediator, or a jury. A reason often given for settling a case is to save the cost and effort of going to trial. Another is to avoid the unpredictability of a jury trial. The parties on both sides are simply too unsure about how jurors will see the facts of a case to undergo the risks of facing a jury.

As a result of so many lawsuits being resolved without ever reaching a jury, only about 0.5 percent of all civil lawsuits filed in America ever come before a jury. The percentage of criminal trials reaching a jury is only slightly higher. Should we be disturbed by this near-abandonment of trial by jury? Are the experts any better than everyday people at trying the facts? There is much more on this later.

In order to prevent overtly biased fact finding among jurors, lawyers in America are given a certain degree of freedom during jury selection to strike, or exclude, jurors who appear at the outset of a trial to be too biased to render an impartial verdict. Such strikes may be for cause, when a potential juror frankly admits that he or she is already leaning strongly toward one side or the other. If the judge agrees that a potential juror is strongly predisposed toward one side or the other, then he or she is struck from the panel.

Strikes may also be peremptory, when an attorney is allowed to remove a certain number of jurors, usually three to six, without having to give a reason. The only limitation on how a lawyer uses peremptory strikes is that the lawyer cannot remove a potential juror from the panel simply because of the potential juror's race or sex. Nevertheless, race and sex seem to influence cause strikes because a juror's race and sex may predict how a juror will interpret the facts of a case.

I was called for jury duty in the Los Angeles Superior Court in spring 2012. The case involved a young Hispanic woman who was allegedly assaulted by her boyfriend. As I sat through the jury selection, I noted that the defense attorney for the alleged assailant used her peremptory strikes to eliminate several young Hispanic women in the jury panel. Apparently, the defense attorney assumed that young Hispanic women would be too sympathetic with the alleged victim and would thus be unable to give the alleged assailant a fair hearing. On the other side, the prosecuting attorney tended to use her peremptory strikes to exclude older Asian men from the jury. The prosecuting attorney may have thought that Asian men would question why the assault victim had gotten herself into such a bad relationship in the first place and had failed to take better care of herself. (Or maybe this is just my story about the prosecuting attorney's story about older Asian men.)

The very practice of allowing cause strikes and peremptory strikes constitutes an implicit acknowledgment by the court that a juror's attitudes and experience can profoundly influence how a juror tries the facts of a case. There is much more to say about fact finding and jury selection later, but at this point, it is enough to note that fact finding is a constructive process. The ambiguous evidence in many lawsuits invites jurors to rely on their life experiences in order to "ascertain the truth about what really occurred."

Chapter Summary

What accounts for people's divergent reactions to the facts of the cases described in this chapter? When every mock juror in the gunshot case heard the same evidence, why would some find a restaurant owner responsible for the accidental discharge of a gun in an off-duty employee's backpack, while others saw the tragedy as a random fluke? How could a real trial jury find McDonald's responsible for burns from spilled coffee and award millions of dollars in damages, when much of the public saw the verdict as ludicrous? You may have wondered how apparently reasonable adults could have reached verdicts so different from what appears so obvious to you. "Were those people crazy?" you might be asking.

As this book argues over the following chapters, supplying facts when they are ambiguous and interpreting facts when they are seemingly clear is not arbitrary. It generally reflects a juror's best efforts to piece together what likely happened, given the juror's worldviews and life experiences, which serve to filter the facts. It also reflects built-in biases in the human brain, which lead jurors to construct stories and make quick decisions. This built-in tendency, in turn, explains why many jurors lean toward one side or the

CHAPTER TWO

Supplying Facts in Early Juries

Constructing or interpreting facts based on a juror's own experience is not unusual in the history of the jury. For most of the millennium during which some form of jury trial has existed in England, and then in America, trials were brief, evidence was scant, and deliberations often lasted just a few minutes. Under such circumstances, jurors were expected, or forced, to rely on their personal experiences in order to render a rapid verdict.

In the earliest days of trial by jury, jurors did not try the facts at all; they supplied the facts. A jury in twelfth-century England was no more than a "body of neighbors summoned by some public officer to give upon oath a true answer to some questions."[1] A typical question in a criminal trial might be, "Did John, the tanner, act in self-defense when he killed William, the stableman?" "Did Robert, the mill owner, lie in wait in order to slay Allan, the farmer, because of a quarrel?" Or, "Did Richard, the carter, deliberately run down Geoffrey, the son of Roger, with his wagon, because Geoffrey would not yield the road?" In a civil trial, typical questions involved debts, boundary disputes, and unfilled obligations. Who owed what to whom?

To answer such questions, a group of men—never women—was assembled from villages near where the incident took place. The jurors usually came from the same or not much higher social rank than the accused person. They might range from "gentlemen and knights" to men of the "middling sort"— yeomen, farmers, tradesmen, and artisans.[2] Most important, the jurors were expected to have personal knowledge about the "neighborhood." What was going on in town? Who were the cast of characters? What were their quirks and habits? How believable was the defendant? What was his reputation? What had jurors heard about the case?

According to Thomas Green, a scholar of early juries, "very little is known about what transpired after the jury was sworn in."[3] But available records suggest that the following situation was fairly typical:

> The defendant stood at the bar in sight of both judge and jury; he stood alone; unaccompanied by counsel or friend. The sheriff or other official repeated the charges, then fell back, leaving the defendant to face the bench. No witnesses could come forward either for or against him; the self-informed jurors were the witnesses for good or ill. . . . Jurors were influenced as much by the defendant's reputation and social position as by the act with which he had been charged. . . . Fact finding involved an assessment of personal worth: Was the suspect the sort of person likely to have committed a certain act with malice? And almost inevitably trial jury verdicts came to be judgments about who ought to live and who ought to die, not merely determinations regarding who did what to whom and with what intent.[4]

A rare example of an actual jury trial from 1291 was reported by the British legal historian William Maitland:

> Henry had been found dead and a knife was nearby. John Miller was arrested because he was the last person seen with Henry, but John denied even knowing the deceased. . . . Twelve jurors were asked for their verdict. They concluded under oath that because John denied any association with Henry or any knowledge of him, and the jurors knew this to be false, and further because Henry went out in John's company but did not return, they understand that he is guilty.[5]

Another thirteenth-century murder trial is interesting because of its close resemblance to a twentieth-century murder trial that provided the facts for a body of research known as the story model of jury decision making, described in the next chapter. In 1292, a man named Alan de la More killed a man named John Tyrel. The jury's task was to decide if the murder happened in self-defense. Here is the evidence that they heard:

> Alan and John had argued until John ran home to fetch a sword. Alan, seeing John approaching, and desiring to evade John's malicious intent, kept himself underneath the horse his father, Robert, was riding. Robert did all in his power to prevent John from striking Alan, but John chased Alan into a certain corner, where as a last resort, Alan retaliated with a mortal blow. The court asked whether Alan could have fled before John returned from his house armed. The jury replied that Alan could not have fled because John was faster than he.[6]

Because the jury knew John to be faster than Alan, they decided that Alan could not have fled. Thus, Alan's mortal blow to John must have been an act of self-defense. Alan was acquitted.

The Self-Informing Jury

As these examples show, medieval jurors were self-informing. No evidence was presented at court. The evidence came from jurors' own experience with the accused person, the person's reputation in the neighborhood, and the circumstances surrounding the alleged crime or dispute. In the village of Stratford in 1199, a man was accused of killing a child with an arrow. At his trial, the man said the child's death was an accident. The jurors knew the accused party well enough to decide that he had no reason or intent to shoot an arrow deliberately at a child. The jurors agreed with the man's explanation that the death was an accident, and they quickly found him not guilty.[7]

Even though evidence was not presented at court in these early trials, the jurors could and often would gather their own evidence. Because jurors were summoned several days before the trial date, they could talk to villagers, seek out friends or enemies of the accused, and arm themselves with local gossip. Once jurors arrived at the trial court, they could confer with others who had been summoned for jury duty. They would also be lobbied by people who wanted to tell one side of the story or the other. So, while jurors were technically self-informing, their information about the facts of a dispute may have come from a variety of sources, in addition to their own experience with the accused.[8]

Sometimes medieval jurors were privately informed or preinformed or informally informed by people with an interest in the trial outcome. Over time, these informal presentations became so elaborate that, in 1412, a number of prospective jurors were brought together for dinner on a Saturday night before the trial in order to listen to representatives of the plaintiff and defendant "show their evidences." To sweeten the pot, each potential juror also received a fish or two.[9]

Early jurors not only supplied their own trial facts or were preinformed about trial facts, but they also were not above altering known facts or ignoring facts in order to justify a verdict they wished to reach. A fourteenth-century inquest in an English village charged that a man named Robert Bousserman came home to his cottage for lunch and found his wife having sexual intercourse with a man named John Dougherty. Robert grabbed his hatchet and killed John with a swift strike to the head. Although English law at the time did not permit a man to kill another man for cuckoldry, the law did allow a homeowner to slay a trespasser. In order to justify acquitting the murderous husband, the jury who heard the case fabricated a story. According to the jury's revised story, the murder happened, not at midday, but at night. Under the cloak of darkness, the murder victim broke into the assailant's cottage, where the defendant's wife slipped out of her bed as her husband slept. Her husband awoke, discovered the trespasser, and killed him. The trial record describes the jury's verdict this way:

> John Dougherty came at night to the house of Robert in the village of Laughs-dale as Robert and his wife lay asleep in bed in the peace of the King, and he entered Robert's house; seeing this, Robert's wife secretly arose from her husband and went to John, and John went to bed with Robert's wife; in the meantime Robert awakened and, hearing noise in his house and seeing that his wife had left his bed, sought her in his house and found her with John; immediately John attacked Robert with a knife . . . and wounded him and stood between him and the door of Robert's house continually stabbing and wounding him, and Robert seeing that his life was in danger and that he could no way flee further, in order to save his life he took up a hatchet and gave John one blow to the head.[10]

Reinterpreting the facts of a case, as the jury here did, was not unusual in medieval England. Local villagers tended to be more lenient than the king's officers, who brought an accused criminal to trial and presented the official perspective on the facts of the crime. If it took revising the facts in order to spare a local man's life, then jurors were often more than willing to construct an alternative version that avoided the death penalty.

The Witness-Informed Jury

By the mid-fifteenth century, self-informed juries were giving way to witness-informed juries and instructional trials. The calamitous fourteenth-century plague greatly reduced the population of potential jurors in local villages. With fewer potential jurors in the pool, the growing burden of more frequent jury summons made it hard to recruit local villagers for jury duty. As a result, juries were staffed by court officials, bailiffs, coroners, and other official hangers-on. The evidence was presented through oral statements of the accused persons and sometimes their relatives; deeds, contracts, and other official documents were explained by counsel; legal charges were clarified by court officials. By the late fifteenth century, witnesses were so common that one trial record demanded that "either party shall produce . . . witnesses who shall testify . . . all they know concerning the truth of the issue about which the parties contend."[11]

As witness-informed juries gradually replaced self-informed juries,

> the job of a juror evolved into something that a modern lawyer, and a modern juror, would recognize without much difficulty. Jurors listened to evidence and "used their common sense to figure out what really happened and whether the law had been violated." Sometimes they followed their own understanding of the law rather than the court's, and they frequently were more lenient toward lawbreakers than the statutes required. But for good or for ill, the jury system had its roots in a popular institution in which men of several ranks shared the task of judging.[12]

When English colonists came to America, they carried with them the English legal custom of a witness-informed jury. With slight variations, the charters of each of the original colonies provided for some form of trial by jury, with testimony by witnesses. However, in colonies that were founded by people fleeing religious persecution in England, jurors were expected to base their verdicts not only on the facts but also on their religious beliefs. An example of such a trial appears in the diary of the governor of Plimoth Plantation, which records a trial in 1642 of an adolescent male servant who was tried for "buggery." The young man was indicted for buggering a "mare, a cow, two goats, five sheep, two calves, and a turkey." After a speedy public trial with a judge and jury, the jury returned a verdict requiring death for the young man and for each of the animals as well, "according to the law, Leviticus XX, 15."[13]

Colonial American juries also departed from weighing the facts as they were stated by the king's officers for political reasons. When jury trials were brought under English law, or the "Crown's Law," which pertained to the colonies chartered by the king of England, jurors often reached verdicts that expressed their dissatisfaction with English rule. In one famous case, a man named Peter Zenger published an article in his newspaper the *New York Weekly Journal* that described the English governor of New York as a "Large Spaniel . . . that has lately strayed from his Kennel . . . with his Mouth full of fulsome Panegyricks . . . to abuse Mankind by imposing a great many Falsehoods upon them." So offended was the governor by this description that he charged Mr. Zenger with "false, malicious, seditious, scandalous libel." Under the king's law, such an irreverent depiction of the king's representative was indeed considered "seditious libel." Nevertheless, it took a jury of New York colonists only a short while to ignore the king's law and return a verdict of not guilty.[14]

Brief Trials and Speedy Deliberations

Unlike today's trials, such as the four-month-long, forty-witness Dewey & LeBouef trial, whose jury deadlocked after three weeks of deliberations, jury trials in the early-modern period were typically very brief, even into the nineteenth century. Trials seldom involved lawyers. There was no examination or cross-examination of witnesses. And deliberations often took no longer than a few minutes.

Throughout the fifteenth century, trial jurors were commonly forbidden to have food or drink in order to speed up trials. According to one commentator, "The rule against food and drink kept common law litigation humming along with almost indecent haste. By this means a pair of justices could get through several trials in a single day."[15] Perhaps this scenario explains eighteenth-century English poet Alexander Pope's skepticism of the jury system when he wrote, "Wretches hang that jury men may dine."[16]

Even when the rule against food and drink was relaxed, jury trials still proceeded at what for us seems an almost unbelievably fast clip. In the summer of 1751, for example, a jury in Surrey, England, convened at 7:00 a.m. on a Saturday. First came an infanticide case, followed by trials involving a series of robberies and crimes against property, such as stealing a loaf of bread. By 2:00 in the afternoon, when the jury broke for an early dinner, the jury had heard and rendered verdicts in ten separate cases. At 5:00 p.m., the jury reconvened to hear six more cases. After resting on Sunday, the same jury spent Monday, Tuesday, and Wednesday hearing an additional thirty-seven cases. In all, the jury heard fifty-three cases in the span of four days. Often the jury would not stop to deliberate after each case, waiting instead to sort out several cases in one sitting. Some verdicts even involved the death sentence.[17]

American trials during this period likewise tended to be brief, with the jury hearing several cases and rendering several verdicts in a single day. As late as the 1890s, court records in Tallahassee, Florida, indicate that the average trial took a half-hour or less. This process was described by historians who examined the Florida court records:

A jury was hurriedly thrown together. Case after case paraded before them. The complaining witness told his story; sometimes another witness or two told his story; sometimes another witness or two appeared; the defendant also told his story, with or without any witnesses; the lawyers (if any) spoke; the judge charged the jury. The jury retired, voted and returned. Then the court went immediately to the next case on the list.[18]

The same type of jury trials occurred in New York City in the late nineteenth century. According to a Stanford Law School professor, a typical New York criminal trial looked like this:

> First of all, there was no voir dire proceeding. Twelve men were impaneled, quite quickly and without much hullabaloo; and they sat for not one but a whole series of trials. In most trials the defendant had no lawyer at all. The trial, from start to finish, was over in a day. Many trials were over within an hour. The jury spent very little time before reaching a verdict. There was little or no cross-examination—nobody raised objections—certainly not in the lawyer-less cases—and the niceties of due process or the law of evidence were not rigorously observed. Trials were hasty and short, in other words, quick and dirty, even slapdash.[19]

Under such circumstances, jurors certainly would not have been able to weigh the facts of individual cases very carefully. With so little evidence, the best they could do would have been to summon up from memory whatever they knew about the types of disputes being tried and the types of people involved in such disputes. Then the jurors would have reasoned from their own experience about what was likely to have happened, why it must have happened, and who should be held responsible. Jurors basically voted their biases. Deliberations would have been little more than announcements of what individual jurors had already decided before they retired to deliberate.

A Celebrated Nineteenth-Century American Jury Trial

In the unusual trial when the niceties of due process and the law of evidence were observed, jurors still filtered the facts through their own peculiar lenses and spent little time deliberating. In 1818, for example, a jury in New York City was convened to answer the question "Is a whale a fish?"[20] It seems that the New York legislature passed a law requiring salesmen of fish oils to ensure that their casks had been inspected and certified to contain only fish oil and no adulterations. The inspection added an extra "inspector's fee" to the cost of the oil. A candlemaker who bought three casks of whale oil from a purveyor refused to pay the inspector's fee. He claimed that a whale is not a fish, and because the inspection tax pertained only to fish oil, he owed no fee. The fish oil provider sued the candlemaker to force him to pay the inspector's fee. At stake was nothing less than nineteenth-century natural science; the natural order of living creatures; and modern taxonomy's view that a whale is a mammal, not a fish.

A celebrated trial ensued. Over the course of two days, famous natural-ists, scientists, whalers, and merchants testified about the nature and status of whales. The trial received a great deal of attention in the national and international press because the citizens of New York were being asked to legislate the order of nature. At the end of the two-day trial, twelve jurymen retired to deliberate. Fifteen minutes later, they returned with their verdict. The candlemaker who ordered whale oil did indeed owe the fish oil purveyor his rightful inspector's fee. Whale oil is fish oil, the jury decreed. None of the jurors was interviewed after the verdict was rendered, so no one knows why the jury reached this verdict or why the jury announced its verdict so quickly. The New York press argued that the jurors relied on "common sense" and "common usage"; a whale is obviously a fish. Boston and Philadelphia papers derided New York's "philistine culture." Other commentators labeled the verdict a victory for religion and tradition over science.

Historian of science Graham Burnett, in his analysis of this trial *Trying Leviathan*, offers an explanation more within the perspective of this book. The jurors reached their verdict, he explains, by constructing and interpret-ing facts in light of their personal experiences. The trial involved the claims of at least four different "communities": "university trained natural philoso-phers, practical whale-men, businesslike men of affairs, and 'everyone else,' the ordinary English speakers of New York." Each of these groups represented a different "social class, guild, and geography."[21] Because the jurors were drawn from New York's "everyone else" community, they reached a verdict that "everyone else" could understand. Relying on common sense and their own experience, they quickly decided that a whale is a fish and the inspec-tor's fee for fish oil should apply equally to whale oil, case over. This trial suggests that, as late as the nineteenth century, witness-informed juries who heard testimony from highly regarded naturalists and "men of affairs" quickly devolved into self-informed juries when they retired to deliberate.

Chapter Summary

The history of jury fact finding has always been more or less a constructive process. The known facts of a case, whether supplied by jurors, gathered from hearsay, or presented through witnesses, become the elements of a story that jurors rapidly constructed in order to make sense out of what seems to have happened in a dispute.

In the past, this intuitive process worked fairly efficiently. Jurors relied on their intuitions and life experience to reach a verdict quickly, even render-ing several verdicts in a single day, as this chapter demonstrates. Such quick, intuitive verdicts were accepted by the court and community because the jurors were similar to the population they represented and often similar to the people they sentenced or acquitted. Jurors could empathize with circumstances that might plausibly explain a crime and lead to a dispute—or not. Consensus verdicts were easier to achieve and faster to hand down.

The human brain is pretty good at this type of reasoning, as the next chapter shows. Jumping to conclusions from limited evidence and explaining new events by comparing them to similar events from a person's own life is how the brain evolved to function. But this built-in, hard-wired process does not work as well in today's complex litigation. As evidence has become more complicated and trials now go on for weeks or months and juries grow more diverse, the human brain has failed to change accordingly. The brain still jumps to conclusions based on limited evidence, still draws on familiar stories to understand new material, and still tends to ignore or reinterpret facts that do not fit the convenient stories. Different types of people, from different backgrounds, with different life experiences, tell different stories, which further complicates the process. This is why a judge's instructions "to weigh all of the evidence, to avoid making a decision until all of the evidence is heard, to ignore evidence not presented in court, and to reason together to reach a unanimous decision" are routinely, if unconsciously, disobeyed.

With little evidentiary foundation, today's jurors construct stories about how guns happen to fire in fast food restaurants, about the proper temperature at which coffee should be served at a drive-up window, and about why a sleeping mother may not have heard her dying child's cries as a power window pressed against the child's neck. Similar stories were constructed almost a thousand years ago to explain a homeowner's murderous response to a domestic intruder in an English village.

The next chapter explores in more detail how the human brain functions in the courtroom and whether it can be trained to function differently. The following chapters consider how trial information can be presented differently and whether alternatives to the jury trial might better serve justice in America.

CHAPTER THREE

How Jurors Use Facts to Tell Stories

The single-most revealing program of psychological research on how jurors reach a verdict was conducted during the 1970s using the details of an actual murder trial in Boston, Massachusetts. Much like a trial from thirteenth-century England, the question for jurors to decide was whether the murderer acted in self-defense. The case was *Commonwealth of Massachusetts v. Johnson*, and the basic evidence was as follows:

On the afternoon of May 9, 1976, a man named Alan Caldwell and a man named Frank Johnson both happened to be drinking in a working-class Boston bar called Gleason's Grill. According to the bartender, the two men had a quarrel. Mr. Caldwell, who was six feet, two inches tall and weighed more than two hundred pounds, threatened the smaller Mr. Johnson with a straight razor. At that point, Mr. Johnson left the bar, as did Mr. Caldwell a few minutes later. That evening, around 9:00 p.m., Mr. Johnson returned to the bar with one of his friends. A couple hours later, at about 11:00 p.m., Mr. Caldwell showed up. Shortly afterward, the two men stepped outside together.

The bartender said he could see through the window that a fight broke out between the two men, but he missed the details of the fight because a large neon sign partially blocked his view. Mr. Johnson's friend said he watched the fight through the barroom door. The friend said he saw the larger Mr. Caldwell strike the first blow. Then he said Mr. Caldwell pulled a straight razor out of his pocket, and Mr. Johnson drew a knife. The two men scuffled, and Mr. Caldwell fell to the ground.

A police officer patrolling his beat heard the commotion, approached the men, and testified that he saw Mr. Caldwell strike Mr. Johnson. The officer said Mr. Johnson then drew a knife and stabbed Mr. Caldwell in the chest. The officer's view of the two men may have been partially blocked by a parked car, however, according to a barmaid who was on duty that evening.

The officer said he disarmed Mr. Johnson, arrested him, and took him to the police station, while Mr. Caldwell's body was removed by an ambulance. The medical examiner who performed an autopsy testified that Mr. Caldwell had a blood alcohol level of .32 percent, which indicated that he was intoxicated.

When Mr. Johnson took the stand at trial, he recounted the events of that day, starting in the afternoon. He said Mr. Caldwell threatened him with a razor because Mr. Caldwell misunderstood an exchange between Mr. Johnson and a woman at the bar. Mr. Johnson said he left the bar to avoid trouble and spent the afternoon and early evening with his wife and six children. When his friend stopped by at about 9:00, Mr. Johnson said they decided to go to Gleason's Grill to have a nightcap. After a while, Mr. Caldwell showed up and, according to Mr. Johnson, asked Mr. Johnson to step outside for a conversation. Once outside, Mr. Johnson said, Caldwell became hostile, threatened to kill him, and punched him in the face. As Mr. Johnson stumbled away, he said he saw Caldwell draw a straight razor. Johnson said he then drew his fishing knife, which he usually carried on his person so that it would be out of reach of his children. Mr. Johnson said that Mr. Caldwell ran onto the knife as he came at Mr. Johnson one more time.

During cross-examination, the prosecution questioned whether Mr. Johnson did in fact usually carry his fishing knife in his pocket or whether he went home to get it before returning to the bar. The prosecution also questioned the details of the fight, especially whether Mr. Caldwell ran against Mr. Johnson's knife or Mr. Johnson stabbed Mr. Caldwell. The prosecution called for a verdict of first-degree murder. The defense said Mr. Johnson acted in self-defense. The judge instructed the jurors to "put away all prejudices, determine what actually happened from the evidence presented" and be the "sole judges of the truth."

The Story Model for Jury Decision Making

In order to study how jurors reached a verdict on this case, two psychologists, Nancy Pennington and Reid Hastie, hired actors to reenact the actual trial.[1] The reenactment was filmed and shown to a group of volunteers from the Massachusetts Superior Court jury pool. Each volunteer was instructed to watch the film, "be one of the jurors," and try to reach a verdict. While watching the film, each volunteer was told to "talk out loud" to an associate of the researchers about their reactions to the trial. They were also asked questions about the evidence presented. Jurors' comments were then transcribed into a written format and analyzed by the psychologists.

The first thing the psychologists noted was that almost all the jurors tended to make up stories as they watched the filmed reenactment of the murder trial. The stories contained episodes that linked the characters' motives and actions in a causal chain, such as "Johnson was angry, so he decided to kill Caldwell." Or "Johnson was afraid, so he armed himself with a knife." Although Mr. Johnson's and Mr. Caldwell's mental states, such as anger or fear, were never mentioned as part of the evidence, they were inferred by the volunteers in order to make the story episode complete. Like jurors in medieval England, these Massachusetts volunteer jurors supplied absent "facts" in order to make sense of what happened.

More surprising than the finding that jurors turned evidence into stories while reaching a verdict was the sheer number of comments jurors made about things that were never presented as evidence at all. Almost half of what jurors talked about while they watched the filmed reenactment of the murder trial were events that were never mentioned in the trial testimony. Instead, they were personal associations or inferences that came from the jurors' imaginations in order to fill in the episodes that comprised jurors' stories. For example, jurors would say things like, "Mr. Caldwell was a violent man," and that's why he confronted Mr. Johnson. Or, "Mr. Johnson was humiliated by Caldwell," and that's why he went home to get his knife.

When the psychologists compared the comments of jurors who found Mr. Johnson guilty of first-degree murder versus those who found him not guilty by virtue of self-defense, they discovered that jurors in each group told very different stories. First-degree-murder jurors imagined mental states, motives, and intentions for both characters different from not-guilty jurors.

Jurors who found Mr. Johnson guilty of first-degree murder said things like, "Mr. Johnson was angry after the quarrel in the bar. Because of his anger, Mr. Johnson decided to find Mr. Caldwell and confront him. So Mr. Johnson went home to get his knife and returned to the bar in order to stab Mr. Caldwell." In contrast, jurors who found Mr. Johnson not guilty by virtue of self-defense told quite a different story: "Mr. Caldwell started a fight with Mr. Johnson after the two men had quarreled. During the fight, Mr. Caldwell pulled out a razor. In order to protect himself, Mr. Johnson pulled out his knife, which he usually carried. As the two men scuffled, Mr. Caldwell fell against the knife and received a wound, from which he died." The most important difference between the stories told by the guilty jurors and the not-guilty jurors was the jurors' beliefs about why Mr. Johnson pulled out his knife. In the guilty version, Mr. Johnson pulled out his knife in order to kill Mr. Caldwell. In the not-guilty version, Mr. Johnson pulled out his knife in order to protect himself.

Compare these alternative scenarios with a verdict returned by the rural English jurors in 1292. In that case, after a quarrel between Allan and John, John went home to fetch a sword and returned to confront Allan. Because

Allan could not outrun John, Allan was forced to strike a mortal blow to John in self-defense. The thirteenth-century jurors inferred that John, the victim, was angry and came after Allan, which made Allan, the murderer, afraid. In the thirteenth-century case and in the twentieth-century case, jurors who found the assailant not guilty used the same reasoning and told similar stories, even though the trials are separated by eight hundred years.

Another study conducted by Pennington and Hastie shows how jurors' stories about a case influence which facts they believe were presented in the evidence.[2] In this study, college students read a written version of the Caldwell–Johnson murder trial and were told to reach a verdict. After reaching a verdict, the students were given a memory test, supposedly to see how well they could recall the evidence that was presented in the trial. The students were instructed to check off every item in a long list of statements that they remembered reading in the transcript. The memory test was constructed, however, so that, in addition to actual statements from the transcript, it included statements that never appeared in the transcript.

When the memory test was scored, it showed that the college students remembered different statements from the list depending on the verdict they reached. Those students who reached a guilty verdict remembered more statements that supported their verdict, such as, "Johnson stabbed Caldwell in the chest," than statements that did not support their verdict. The students also remembered reading statements that were never actually present in the transcript, such as "Johnson was looking for Caldwell." Similarly, students who reached a not-guilty verdict remembered more statements from the list that supported their verdicts, such as "Johnson held his knife out in front of himself." Like their guilty counterparts, they also falsely remembered reading statements that were never present in the transcript but that supported their not-guilty verdicts, such as "Johnson was trying to protect himself."

How Stories Influence Verdicts

Having established that jurors intuitively construct stories in order to reach a verdict, that jurors remember more evidence in support of their verdicts than evidence contradicting their verdicts, and that jurors manufacture additional evidence never presented in order to fill in their stories, Pennington and Hastie took their research a step further. If stories are so crucial to jurors' verdicts, they reasoned, then maybe trial evidence would be more persuasive if it was presented as a story instead of as a series of statements made by witnesses under examination on the witness stand.

To test this proposition, the psychologists made a tape recording of one hundred statements taken directly from the transcript of the

Caldwell–Johnson trial proceedings.[3] Fifty statements supported the prosecution's case, and fifty supported the defense's case. More than a hundred college students were asked to listen to the tape recordings and render a verdict, either guilty or not guilty. In one version of this test, the statements were presented in the same order in which they were offered by witnesses over the course of the actual trial. This version was called the "witness order." In another version of the test, the statements were presented in a temporal and causal sequence that matched the occurrence of the real events; that is, as a story. This version was called the "story order."

The findings of this test were striking: When the prosecution's case was presented in story order and the defense's case in witness order, 78 percent of the student jurors favored the prosecution. But when the prosecution's case was presented in witness order and the defense's in story order, then only 31 percent of the student jurors favored the prosecution and reached a guilty verdict. In other words, presenting the trial information in a way that mimicked jurors' intuitive organizing of information into a story enhanced the persuasiveness of the presentation.

If we were able to know what was going through jurors' heads in almost any trial, we would no doubt find a story lurking. Chances are, many aspects of jurors' stories would never have been presented in the evidence. For example, let's go back to the mock trial in chapter 1, where a little girl accidentally stepped on the power-window switch in her mother's car, with tragic consequences. Here are some of the common elements in the stories told by mock jurors who decided the power-window switch's design was not defective:

When the window went up against the little girl's throat, the girl must have screamed and made choking sounds.

The mother didn't hear her daughter's screaming and choking sounds for at least sixty seconds because, when she tried to lower the window, the power had already turned off.

The reason the mother couldn't hear her daughter's screaming and choking for so long was because the mother must have passed out.

The mother must have passed out because she had been drinking.

The mother had been drinking because she had just attended an afternoon soccer game, where the girl's father had played.

If the mother hadn't been drinking and passed out, then she would have heard her daughter choking and would have reached over and pressed the switch to lower the window and save her daughter.

Therefore, the mother was at fault for her daughter's death, not the allegedly defective design of the power-window switch.

In fact, no information was presented to jurors about whether the girl's mother had been drinking. The jurors were told that the window's motor made the window rise when the "up" side of the switch was pressed. The jurors were also told that, if the rising window encountered an obstacle while the "up" side of the switch was pressed, then the window's motor would continue trying to elevate the window for at least sixty seconds, until the motor automatically cut off. Finally, the jurors were informed that, when the mother woke up and attempted to press the power-window switch to lower the window and free her daughter, the motor had already shut off, and the window would not go down. Therefore, the jurors knew that at least a minute had to have passed before the mother woke up and tried to rescue her daughter from the window's grip.

The jurors needed an explanation for why the mother made no attempt to rescue her daughter for more than a minute, a minute that the jurors assumed was filled with the girl's screaming, crying, and choking. In order to explain this gap in time, the jurors filled in information. The mother had to have passed out from drinking, the jurors' reasoned. What else could explain her failure to respond to her daughter's assumed distress cries?

Note that this story links a premise, the mother's assumed intoxication, with a consequence, the little girl's choking. The story has a beginning (attending a soccer game), a middle (resting in the car with the battery power on), and an end (the girl's death). The story also involves a number of episodes in order to get from beginning to end. It is a coherent, compelling story that explains a tragic event. It produces a conclusion and, thus, a verdict.

How Jurors' Stories Begin

Pennington and Hastie would point out that, in order for jurors to tell this story, which led to a verdict in favor of the auto manufacturer, they needed to know at least three types of information[4]:

1. **Evidence.** First, jurors needed to know something about the evidence. In this case, jurors needed to know that the design of the power-window switch did not cut off power to the window for more than a minute after the rising glass encountered an obstacle. They also needed to know that, when the mother tried to lower the window, the switch was no longer powered because the mother was unable to lower the window by pressing on the switch. Therefore, the jurors knew that at least a minute passed before the mother attempted to rescue her daughter, who was trapped between the upper edge of the window and the top of the window frame. Pennington and Hastie refer to this type of information as "case-specific information."

2. **World Knowledge.** Second, jurors needed to know something about events from their own lives that are similar to events in the dispute. In this case, jurors had to hold certain beliefs about weekend-afternoon adult soccer games involving Latin Americans, where, the jurors assumed, fans typically drink beer. Pennington and Hastie refer to this type of information as "world knowledge."

3. **Story Structure.** Third, jurors needed to know something about the nature of stories and what makes a story complete. They needed to know intuitively that good stories have a beginning, a middle, and an end: that the mother attended a soccer game; that, after the game, she rested with the car's power on; and that the little girl died when she stepped on the power-window switch and the rising window choked her. Pennington and Hastie refer to this type of information as "generic expectations about story structure."

Taken together, when jurors know something about the evidence in a case, something about events similar to the case, and something about the nature of satisfactory stories, they naturally create a narrative. The stories fill in gaps, explain consequences, and allow jurors to make sense of what happened in the accident. In this case, inferring that people drink beer at soccer games allowed the jurors to explain why the mother did not wake up and rescue her daughter. This fact shifted attention away from the design of the power-window switch to the condition of the mother. It explained the little girl's death and absolved the switch design from fault. The filled-in "fact," that the mother must have been drinking, drove the majority verdict relieving the automaker of responsibility for the girl's death.

A second case involving another sleeping driver and alleged use of alcohol prompted quite a different story among jurors at an actual trial in Santa Fe, New Mexico. A retired English professor from an Ivy League university, who spends the summers in Santa Fe, related the following account of a trial in which he served as jury foreperson:

A middle-aged woman took a plane from Los Angeles, California, to Albuquerque, New Mexico. She landed in the early evening, retrieved her car from the parking garage, and began the drive to her home in El Rito, New Mexico, two hours north. When she was about halfway home, the woman pulled off the highway into the densely wooded town of Tesuque, just north of Santa Fe, to have dinner with a friend. After dinner and a few glasses of wine, the woman began the second hour of the trip back to her home. She drove a few winding miles through the sleepy town before rejoining the main highway. At that point, the woman realized she was feeling tired and a little tipsy, so she pulled off the road to take a nap in her car.

Not long after she fell asleep, the woman was awakened by a police officer rapping on her car window and shining a high-powered flashlight beam into her face. The officer asked her to get out of her car and submit to a field sobriety test. The woman agreed and failed the field sobriety test. The police officer promptly arrested her and took her to the police station, where the woman agreed to submit to a Breathalyzer test, which she also failed. The officer charged the woman with driving while intoxicated and locked her in a jail cell for the evening.

The woman believed she had been treated unfairly and demanded a jury trial. The six-person jury was made up of four women and two men. The defense attorney argued that his client had not been driving while intoxicated because she was sleeping when the officer woke her up. The prosecution replied that the woman had driven several miles from her friend's home to the spot where she pulled off the road to rest. When she woke up, the prosecution argued, the woman was likely to continue the drive to her home on the main highway while intoxicated. Therefore, it was reasonable to arrest her, the prosecution concluded, in order to prevent the woman from endangering other drivers on the highway.

According the foreperson, the deliberations began with each juror writing down on a slip of paper whether they believed the woman was guilty. The initial vote was four for guilty and two for not guilty. One of the four jurors who favored a guilty verdict said her son was an alcoholic, and she knew how dangerous alcohol can be. One of the jurors who favored not guilty was the foreman, who said he had been to lots of parties where he had drunk enough wine to know that he should give his car keys to his wife for the drive home, so he could sleep while she drove. Giving his keys to his wife, he argued, was analogous to the defendant's pulling off the road to sleep instead of driving when she felt tipsy. After a morning's deliberation, the jury returned a unanimous verdict of not guilty.

These two jurors—the woman with an alcoholic son and the professor who was elected foreperson—told different stories based on their personal experiences with alcohol. From the female juror's perspective, the driver who failed a field sobriety test and a Breathalyzer test was a danger to others. From the professor's perspective, the woman did exactly the right thing by pulling off the highway and napping until she felt better about driving. The professor added that no one had seen the woman driving erratically and that, in fact, the woman had been arrested for "sleeping while intoxicated." He ultimately prevailed by persuading the other jurors to accept his story, that the woman did the right thing by pulling off the road to sleep off her tipsy state. In doing so, he convinced other jurors to ignore the threat posed by a drunk driver who might have awakened and driven onto the highway in an intoxicated

state. A later chapter looks at the influence of strong leaders on jury deliberations, but for the time being, this example presents yet another instance of
how jurors' stories can trump trial evidence.

A third case shows how jurors resort to a familiar story when complicated
evidence is difficult to understand. This case involves a minor stake in an oil
and gas lease that was so rich even the minor stake could be worth a fortune.
Thirty years ago, two independent Texas oil men, or "wildcatters," bought
a "grab bag" of oil and gas leases located in the western United States for
$8 million. Among the leases was a fractional interest in the net profits on
the oil and gas beneath thousands of acres of federal land in a western state.
For a long time, the oil and gas were too hard to recover because it was
trapped in layers of rock. But several years ago, when fracking made it easier
to recover gas trapped in rock, the wildcatters' fractional interest in the profits from drilling on the land became extremely valuable.

The wildcatters informed the consortium of large oil companies that had
begun drilling on the land that they, the independent oil men, owned a
minor stake in the profits from the drilling. After initialing trying to buy out
the wildcatters, the oil companies denied that the fractional interest was still
valid and refused to share any profits from the drilling. The wildcatters then
sued the consortium of oil companies who were doing the drilling to obtain
what they believed was their share of the profits.

At this point, the case became extremely complicated. The mineral rights
interest that the wildcatters purchased had traded hands many times since
it was first sold in the mid-1950s, and different sales contracts described the
land differently. The land itself had been bundled and rebundled with other
leases several times, which made it unclear whether the original lease was
still intact. And various contracts, agreements, and lease arrangements could
be interpreted as either invalidating the original fractional profits interest or
reaffirming it. In a mock trial, most jurors found the contracts, lease agreements, and oil rights law hard to understand.

But beneath the arcane property and ownership disputes, a classic, cultural narrative lurked. The independent oil men were facing off with Big Oil.
The wildcatters' ownership of a fractional interest in the profits from oil and
gas production was a lucky fluke. By purchasing a grab bag of random lease
interests, they had won the rights to many millions of dollars in profits. It was
a needle-in-a-haystack treasure hunt, and it paid off big, if the oil companies
could only be vanquished. This highly appealing narrative helped shape the
case in jurors' minds and led to a majority verdict for the wildcatters.

The mock trial also revealed that certain types of jurors were primed
by their life experiences and beliefs to identify with the wildcatters' story.

Compared to jurors who favored the oil companies, the majority of jurors who favored the independent oil men saw themselves as risk takers, harbored suspicions of Big Oil, doubted if they could stand up to powerful outside forces, and tended to be environmentalists. The classic cultural narrative found a natural audience among a majority of jurors, who then interpreted the evidence as favoring the wildcatters.

Chapter Summary

Jurors intuitively tell stories when they hear trial evidence, and storytelling begins very early in a trial. It stems from a juror's own experiences and views on events similar to events in the trial. People remember more evidence that is consistent with their stories than evidence that is inconsistent, even falsely remembering or manufacturing evidence that was never presented.

Evidence is more persuasive when it is presented as a story than as out-of-order witness testimony or a list of points. In order for a story to be persuasive, it must contain certain types of information: first, evidence that provides a clear explanation of trial events; second, world knowledge that may be applied to the evidence; and third, a sense of how stories are structured, with a beginning, middle, and end. With these three elements, jurors are able to construct a satisfactory story about what happened in a case, which leads to a verdict.

In the next chapter, let's turn from *how* jurors construct stories to *why*. The chapter shows that the human brain evolved to favor a narrative explanation of events over rational analysis of evidence. And I consider the implications of this tendency for jury decision making.

CHAPTER FOUR

Why Jurors Prefer Stories over Facts

At this point, you may be saying to yourself, "I see that jurors tell stories that can influence their verdicts." But you might ask, "Can't jurors overcome this tendency to narrate? Can't they stick to the evidence and not fill in missing facts? Can't they obey the judge's instructions and base their verdicts only on the evidence presented at court and not on events from their own lives? Can't they avoid being hooked by a colorful narrative?" You might even add, with some assurance, "That's what I would do, especially if the judge told me to."

The best explanation of why jurors can't help but tell stories comes from Nobel Prize–winning psychologist Daniel Kahneman. In his 2011 book, *Thinking, Fast and Slow*, Kahneman says that the brain works in two distinctly different ways[1]:

1. **System 1 Thinking.** The first and most common way in which the brain works Kahneman calls System 1 thinking. This type of thinking is fast, automatic, and intuitive. It happens with no sense of voluntary control. It is based on impressions and feelings. It links circumstances, events, outcomes, and consequences in a causal chain. It jumps to conclusions based on limited evidence. It tells stories.
2. **System 2 Thinking.** The second and far less common way in which the brain works Kahneman calls System 2 thinking. This type of thinking is slow, orderly, analytical, computational, and statistical. It is voluntary and requires concentration and focused attention. And it is generally deployed to justify and support—not to challenge, correct, or edit—the conclusions of System 1 thinking. As Kahneman points out, System 2 thinking is System 1's "handmaid."

An example of the two types of thinking in operation can be seen in a simple thought experiment. Consider this question and try to guess the answer: How many murders occur in the state of Michigan in one year? This is a difficult question to answer. If you are not a resident of Michigan, then you probably have no clue about the state's murder rate. To solve the problem, you might try to recall the murder rate of the state or city where you reside and somehow extrapolate these statistics to the state of Michigan. The actual number of murders would be hard to determine, though, and you would probably have little confidence in your answer.

Now consider a slightly different version of the "Michigan murder" question: How many murders occur in the city of Detroit in one year? For most people, this question seems much easier to answer. A few years ago, when Detroit was on hard times, many Americans held numerous feelings, judgments, and even mental images associated with the city. Pictures of abandoned skyscrapers, boarded-up factories, empty or burned-out homes, and weedy lots come to mind. Add to that newspaper articles about political scandal, a bankrupt city government, and high unemployment, and it becomes easy to suppose high crime and murder rates. Consequently, most people find it easier to come up with a guess about the number of murders per year in the city of Detroit than in the state of Michigan. And quite illogically, people who are asked to estimate the number of annual murders in Detroit typically guess a higher number than people who are asked to estimate the annual number of murders in the entire state of Michigan!

Kahneman uses the Michigan murder riddle as an example of how the associative operations of System 1 thinking typically overrule the analytical operations of System 2 thinking. Because we have vivid mental associations and images connected with Detroit, we can easily tell a story about crime and murder in that city. In contrast, because most of us have few vivid associations and images about the state of Michigan, we have a much harder time either telling a story or coming up with statistics about the state's murder rate. As Kahneman puts it, "The confidence that individuals have in their beliefs depends mostly on the quality of the story they can tell about what they see, even if they see little." He elaborates, "You build the best possible story from the information available to you, and if it is a good story you believe it. Paradoxically, it is easier to construct a coherent story when you know little, when there are fewer pieces to fit into the puzzle."[2]

Why Are Jurors More Persuaded by Stories Than by Evidence?

According to Kahneman, we have evolution to blame for our reliance on stories to get us through the world. The human organism needs continually to assess how to survive. For example, when a band of early humans camping near a spring heard a rustling noise in the savannah grasses, which sort of assessment had the most survival value? Did it make sense to activate System 2 thinking and carefully calculate the odds that the noise was a burrowing rodent, an unexpected breeze, a harbinger of changing weather? Or was it more adaptive to rely on System 1 thinking, to match the noise with past experiences and associations and quickly decide whether the sound signaled a possible dinner or the threat that one was about to become the dinner of another creature?

Because System 1 thinking is so ingrained and operates so automatically, it cannot be turned off at will, according to Kahneman. Another experiment he cites involved telling a group of college students the average incidence of muggings and robberies in a certain neighborhood of a large city. A second group of similar students received the same information but also read vivid details about a violent mugging and robbery in the neighborhood. After reading the information, both groups of students were asked to estimate the likelihood that a visitor to the neighborhood would be mugged or robbed. Because both groups of students heard the same information about the average incidents of muggings and robberies per year, their estimates of being mugged or robbed should have been identical. But the students who heard the statistical information and also read a vivid description of a violent mugging estimated a much greater likelihood of a visitor being attacked. The students were more influenced by the vivid description of a single mugging than by the statistical incidence of actual muggings and robberies. The image and its associated story trumped the data.

Can people be trained to forego System 1 thinking and employ System 2 thinking when accurate analysis is required? If a judge instructs jurors to pay careful attention to the evidence in a trial, then can jurors set aside storytelling for a more careful evaluation of each side's case? Research conducted by psychologists who wanted to apply Kahneman's ideas to the legal sphere suggests that this shift is almost impossible to carry off.

A series of experiments asked real judges to evaluate the potential danger of housing paroled sex offenders in a group home located in a middle-class community. One group of judges heard information about the offenders' criminal history, presented in vivid narrative terms and using examples and descriptions of sexual assaults from the offenders' criminal records. This approach was intended to trigger System 1 thinking. A second group of judges heard information presented in statistical terms, which sought to predict the odds that the paroled sex offenders would commit future crimes. This approach was intended to trigger System 2 thinking. Which group of judges do you think viewed the paroled sex offenders as more dangerous to the community? If you sided with Kahneman and predicted that judges who read the clinical information saw a greater danger than those who read the statistical information, then you were right. Even with trained judges, System 1 thinking trumped System 2 thinking.[3]

In a related experiment, the same researchers wondered whether some types of people are simply more susceptible to System 1 type, emotional information than to System 2 type, rational or statistical information. To answer this question, the experimenters administered a test that measured how emotional or rational people were in their worldviews. Some people did indeed score significantly higher in emotional approaches to the world, while others scored significantly higher in rational approaches. Yet both types of people rated paroled sex offenders as more dangerous to the community when they read the narrative information rather than the statistical information.

"But," you might protest, "what if people are specifically instructed to slow down and think carefully," as a judge instructs jurors to do? "Won't that make people less susceptible to emotional appeals?" To answer this question, the experimenters asked one group of people to spend time working difficult math problems that required concentration; these were the rationally primed people. Another group was asked to write about their feelings and emotional states; these were the emotionally primed people. It turned out that priming mattered very little. Regardless of whether people had worked math problems or written about their feelings, those who read narrative information about paroled sex offenders saw the parolees as more dangerous than those who had read the statistical information.[4]

Experiments like these suggest that it is quite difficult for most jurors to switch from their everyday mode of System 1 thinking to the much less common and more difficult mode of System 2 thinking simply because they are sitting in the jury box and the judge admonishes them to consider the evidence carefully. Kahneman poses a relevant question for the courtroom: "How can we improve judgments and decisions, both of our own and those of the institutions that we serve and that serve us?" "The short answer," he reluctantly offers, is that "little can be achieved without a considerable investment of effort." With advice that both judges and jurors should heed, he concludes, "The voice of reason may be much fainter than the loud and clear voice of an erroneous intuition, and questioning your intuitions is unpleasant when you face the stress of a big decision."[5]

The Structure of Trials Encourages Storytelling

If storytelling is an everyday occurrence, as Kahneman suggests, then jury trials may offer the perfect storm to encourage System 1 storytelling over System 2 objective analysis. Attorneys spend days, weeks, or even months presenting evidence under strict rules that the court enforces. The evidence is often presented out of order and in fragments, which the juror has to assemble. It is presented through witnesses, who may only know a tiny fraction of the entire picture. And the information is often unfamiliar, complex, and difficult for the jury to understand. These constraints invite jurors to resort to their own idiosyncratic narratives in order to make sense of the evidence.

As if this were not enough, a typical trial begins with two opportunities for the respective attorneys to present a narrative overview of the events and evidence to follow. A skillful attorney can use these opportunities to influence the type of narratives individual jurors may adopt in order to fit the subsequent evidence into a story. To understand how this attorney-driven storytelling works, let's look at how most trials are structured:

- **Voir Dire.** A typical jury trial begins with voir dire, a phrase that literally means "to see, to speak" in old French and that is pronounced "vwah deer" (or in some parts of the country "voy dyre"). In contemporary legal terms, voir dire refers to pretrial jury selection, which is the attorney's opportunity to see and to speak to prospective jurors. This is the time when the attorneys can question members of the jury pool about any biases or preconceived attitudes they may have on issues similar to the case at hand. In order to question prospective jurors about such biases or preconceived attitudes, the attorneys, or sometimes judges, must provide a brief overview of what the trial will be about. In the hands of a skilled attorney, this pre-voir-dire overview can become quite a vivid tale. Because the prospective jurors are asked to reflect on their own experience and report any beliefs or feelings that might bias them against one side or the other, the jurors almost necessarily begin relating the attorney's narrative overview of the upcoming trial to stories from their own pasts. In other words, voir dire evokes and encourages storytelling from prospective jurors. And the attorney who presents the more compelling story can strongly influence jurors' narratives before the trial ever begins.

- **Opening Statements.** The second opportunity attorneys have to cultivate storytelling among jurors is after the jury has been seated and the trial formally begins. At the beginning of a trial, each attorney presents an opening statement to the members of the jury. This is when each attorney tells the jurors what he or she hopes to prove through the evidence that will be presented. Technically, the opening statement is an overview, or a roadmap, of the upcoming evidence, and it usually lasts from a half-hour to an hour and a half. While some attorneys use the opening statement to offer a list of evidence, a clever attorney can weave such a compelling story about the events, actions, and consequences of the case, as seen from a client's perspective, that the opening statement becomes far more than a dry overview of the upcoming evidence. Delivered by a savvy attorney, the opening statement can implant such a vivid, complete, and satisfying story that jurors may begin to make up their minds before they ever hear any evidence or witnesses at all.

The story provided in the opening statement can also influence which aspects of the evidence jurors attend to and how they remember it, as is seen in the experiments conducted on the story model of jury decision making. Consequently, when jurors retire to deliberate, they remember more evidence consistent with the stories they told themselves during the opening statement than evidence that is inconsistent. And they falsely recall or manufacture more evidence consistent with their stories, even if the evidence was never presented. This explains why the story about the evidence leads jurors to begin making up their minds before any evidence is presented.

Applying the Story Model in Opening Statements

In thirty years of work in a jury research firm, I have found repeatedly that the story model is the most persuasive way to present information to juries. Typically, my firm is hired to help attorneys evaluate the strengths and weaknesses of their cases a few months before the case goes to trial. In order to do this, we stage a mock trial. This involves recruiting a large number of people from the vicinity where the trial will be held. These mock jurors match the demographic characteristics of an actual jury panel, and they are paid enough to encourage them to take a sick day or a personal day off from their regular jobs. This ensures that the mock juries are not made up of people who simply have time on their hands and need extra cash; instead, the mock juries are made up of the same people who will serve on a real jury in the vicinity of the trial.

The mock jurors then watch live or videotaped versions of an hour-long summary of each side's case. After viewing the presentations, the jurors fill out lengthy questionnaires, about a half-inch thick, with several hundred questions about their backgrounds and reactions to the information presented in the two, hour-long presentations. The key question is, of course, what is the juror's verdict? Is the defendant liable or not liable for an alleged misdeed, such as the defective design of an automobile power-window switch or an off-duty restaurant employee's loitering with a concealed handgun?

When we report the results of a mock trial to our client, we first describe the strengths and weaknesses of the client's case in the eyes of the mock jurors, and we report the verdict. Then, we propose a revised jury strategy, which we test in a subsequent mock trial with a new group of jurors. Part of our proposal for a revised jury strategy usually involves turning the client's presentation into a story. Almost always, in the first round of research, the client's attorneys present the facts of the case as they have been trained to do in law school. Typically, the attorneys recite a long list of upcoming evidence, such as witnesses' statements or engineers' testimony or contract language, in a fairly dry, legalistic way. In our office, we refer to this as the yellow-pad approach. It's as though the attorneys write down a hundred statements on a yellow pad and then check off each statement, one by one, as they relay them to the jurors.

In our revised jury strategy, we often write out a twenty-page trial narrative that tells the client's case not as a list of points to be checked off but as a story with a beginning, middle, and end. We provide a set of story themes that preview and organize the evidence in a coherent way. When we run the second round of research, we keep the opposing side's case the same as in the first round, but we replace the client's yellow-pad presentation with our own narrative version of the case. Then we compare the mock jurors' verdicts in the first round, when the client's attorney offered a yellow-pad approach, with jurors' verdicts in the second round, when we substituted a narrative approach for the yellow-pad approach. If the story model research is valid, then the narrative approach should yield a higher verdict share for the client than the yellow-pad approach. This is an easy comparison to make.

Searching through our files we found sixty-seven cases in the last ten years where we ran two successive rounds of research. The cases dealt with all sorts of disputes—consumer products, contracts, automotive design, financial fraud, drugs, medical devices, industrial equipment, and others. Admittedly, the comparison between the first-round, yellow-pad opening statement and the second-round, narrative opening statement is not as controlled as it would be in a formal psychological experiment. The cases were all different. Sometimes the attorneys who hired us presented our narratives word for word; other times they liberally substituted their own words for our narratives while following the general outline; and occasionally they ignored our narratives. Despite this wide variation in how closely the attorneys followed our advice and presented our narratives, when we compared the verdict share achieved by the yellow-pad approach versus the verdict share obtained by our narrative openings, we found that, 72 percent of the time, the narrative approach obtained a larger verdict share than the yellow-pad approach. The largest gain in verdict share was 45 percent, while the smallest was 2 percent. The average gain in verdict share from the narrative approach was 13 percent. Our own experience then clearly confirms the research finding that the story model is a more persuasive way to present trial information than the witness-order approach or the yellow-pad approach.

How Narrative Opening Statements
Influence the Final Verdict

"All right," you might concede, "a narrative opening statement may be more persuasive than an opening statement that merely lists the upcoming evidence or introduces a series of witnesses. But there's a lot more to a trial than the opening statements. There's each side's evidence, presented through witnesses who are examined and cross-examined for hours or even days. Then there are the closing arguments, where each side's attorney reviews all the evidence, often quite emotionally. Next, there are jury deliberations. And finally, the verdict. So, how can a narrative opening statement, however persuasive it may be, have much impact on the verdict?" Should you have raised such a question, you would be probing one of the most intriguing and least understood issues in jury research.[6] Is it likely that a narrative opening statement can be so persuasive that it influences how jurors hear the evidence from both sides over the course of days, weeks, or months of a trial? Is the verdict that a juror favors after the opening statements the same verdict that a jury returns to when the trial is over? In other words, can a trial be won after the opening statements, especially if the opening presents a vivid narrative?

Almost fifty years ago, some of the very first scholars to study jury behavior, Harry Kalven Jr. and Hans Zeisel, published a still-influential book called *The American Jury*. In this book, the authors propose that, in the great majority of cases, the jury's decision is indeed made long before the final phase of the decision process.[7] Exactly how long before the final phase, however, the authors fail to say because they lacked the relevant data. They also published their conclusions well before the story model of jury decision making demonstrated the power of a narrative opening statement. And in a later commentary, Dr. Zeisel acknowledges that it would be difficult to design research that could determine when most jurors begin to make up their minds on a final verdict.[8]

Fortunately, my firm's experience conducting mock trials provided an ideal means of measuring the opening statement's impact on the final verdict. One type of jury exercise we conduct is called a summary trial, which usually lasts two or three full days. On the first morning of the summary trial, each side's attorney presents an opening statement. Both opening statements are crafted as forty-five-minute narratives, with the evidence organized around a story with five themes (about which there is more in a later chapter). After the opening statements, each side gets two to three hours to summarize the evidence in its case. Depending on the case, this involves showing mock jurors videotaped interviews with people in the conflict, video clips of witnesses, graphic diagrams, engineering documents, copies of contracts, testimony from expert witnesses, and projections of future losses allegedly suffered. Following the summary of each side's evidence, the attorney for each side presents a closing argument that reviews the evidence and tells the jurors why they should favor one side over the other. Then the jurors retire to deliberate for several hours, until they reach a verdict or become deadlocked.

Along the way, we ask jurors to provide a "running verdict," telling us which side they think should win at several points in the trial: after both opening statements, after the plaintiff's presentation of its key evidence, after the defendant's presentation of its key evidence, after both closing arguments, and after deliberations. This amounts to obtaining five separate verdicts over the course of the mock trial.

Comparing these five verdicts shows how the percentage of jurors who favor each side's case shifts over the course of the trial. Regardless of each side's verdict share after the opening statements, the majority of jurors almost always shifts in favor of the plaintiff after the plaintiff's presentation of evidence. Then, after the defendant's presentation of its evidence, the majority invariably shifts toward the defense. Finally, after the closing arguments, the percentage of jurors favoring each side usually returns to within a few percentage points of the verdict after the opening statements. Interestingly, although some jurors change their minds during deliberations and publicly side with the majority in order to reach a unanimous verdict, they reveal privately in their questionnaires that they never really changed their minds at all; they just acquiesced with the majority in order to end the deliberations and go home.

To test the strength of this propensity—that a juror's verdict after the closing arguments approximates a juror's verdict after the opening statements—we looked at jurors' verdicts in every summary trial we have run over the past ten years. We categorized the trials by case type, such as automotive-design issues, accounting and auditing issues, or contract disputes, for example. We calculated each side's verdict share at the five key points in the mock trial: (1) after both opening statements, (2) after the plaintiff's presentation of evidence, (3) after the defendant's presentation of evidence, (4) after the closing arguments, and (5) after deliberations. Then we averaged the cases in each category together and compared the verdict shares across each of these five points. Here's what we found:

- **Auto Cases.** Of 18 automotive-design cases, including 851 jurors, 62 percent of jurors favored the defendant after the opening statements had been delivered. The defendant's verdict share then plummeted after jurors heard the plaintiff's damning evidence. After the defendant presented its case, the defendant's verdict share spiked back up to well above 62 percent. But after the closing arguments, the defendant's average verdict share across the eighteen cases once again stood at 62 percent. The defendant's average verdict share after closing arguments was the same as after the opening statements.

- **Accounting Cases.** Of six accounting and auditing cases, including 281 jurors, 57 percent of jurors favored the defendant after the opening statements had been delivered. Once again, the defendant's share dropped after jurors heard the plaintiff's evidence and then spiked significantly after the defendant presented its own evidence. But at the end of the day, the defendant's verdict share was 51 percent, just 6 percent lower than the verdict share after the opening statements.

- **Contract Cases.** Of four contract dispute cases, including 209 jurors, 66 percent of jurors favored the defendant after the opening statements had been delivered. Then, as in the auto and the accounting cases, the defendant's verdict share dropped when jurors heard the plaintiff's evidence and rebounded when they heard the defendant's evidence. But at the end of the trial, after closing arguments, the defendant's verdict share was 63 percent, just 3 percent smaller than after the opening statements.

When we probed more deeply in order to explain why the defendant's verdict share remained so constant after the opening statements and after the closing arguments, we found something interesting: Most of the jurors who lined up with the defendant after the closing arguments were the same people who had lined up with the defendant after the opening statements. In fact, about 80 percent of the jurors in these examples reached the same verdict at the end of the trial as they did at the very beginning. This analysis provides strong support for the view that a majority of jurors begin to make up their minds about who should win and who should lose a lawsuit long before deliberations, in fact as early as the opening statements. It confirms the power of a narrative opening statement. And it suggests that the stories jurors adopt early in a trial influence their perceptions of the evidence.

Chapter Summary

The narrative approach of System 1 thinking is much more automatic and ingrained than is the analytical approach of System 2 thinking. This makes it very hard for people to shift from System 1 thinking to System 2 thinking, even if they are instructed by a judge to pay close attention to the evidence and nothing but the evidence.

Jury trials present situations that strongly encourage narrative-style System 1 thinking. Trials typically begin with competing narratives, often in the form of pre-voir-dire case overviews and then opening statements, both of which allow storytelling by attorneys and invite storytelling by the jurors. In turn, opening statements are more persuasive when they are presented in a narrative format than a non-narrative format. And narrative opening statements lead jurors to begin leaning toward a verdict very early in a trial.

Having established in the first four chapters that jurors can't help but tell stories when they try the facts at a trial, let's turn in the following chapters to consider how jurors' storytelling can be better managed over the course of trials. I first examine jury selection in chapters 5 and 6 and how attorneys can be more or less successful at weeding out people who may tell stories that could bias their perceptions of the evidence. Then in chapter 7, I turn to trial presentations and explore how attorneys can adapt to the brain's propensity to tell stories by offering evidence in a narrative format. After, in chapters 8 and 9, I focus on jury deliberations, both to understand how storytelling shapes deliberations and to see how jurors themselves can make deliberations more effective.

CHAPTER FIVE

Jury Selection

Identifying Who Will Tell Which Stories

If jurors tell stories during trials and if jurors' stories influence the verdicts they reach, then picking a jury should be about picking storytellers. Which type of storyteller will be most and least sympathetic with each side's evidence in a specific case? How can biased storytellers be identified and removed from the jury in order to ensure a fairer trial?

A vivid example of how jury selection affects trial verdicts comes from a highly publicized Florida murder trial that went before a jury in June 2013. Like a murder trial from thirteenth-century England, and very similar to the 1970s Massachusetts murder trial that underpinned the story model of jury decision making, this trial hinged on whether a murder was committed in self-defense. Did a neighborhood-watch patrolman George Zimmerman shoot unarmed African American teenager Trayvon Martin because Mr. Zimmerman feared for his life after he confronted the young man as a suspected prowler? The trial attracted huge publicity, given the racial issues involved, which foreshadowed more recent trials about police shootings of young African American males. President Obama even weighed in on the Zimmerman trial, saying, "If I had a son, he would look like Trayvon." In a controversial verdict, a six-woman jury acquitted Mr. Zimmerman of fatally shooting the unarmed teenager. Let's look at the evidence and then consider the role the jury-selection process may have played in this verdict.

On the evening of February 26, 2012, in Sanford, Florida, just north of Orlando, a seventeen-year-old African American male named Trayvon Martin left a townhouse in a gated community called the Retreat at Twin Lakes in order to buy a snack at a nearby 7-Eleven. The young man, who went to North Miami-Dade High School, was visiting his father and his father's fiancé. He walked twenty minutes in a light rain to reach the store

45

and, as shown on the 7-Eleven's security camera, purchased a bag of Skittles and an Arizona Watermelon Fruit Juice drink. Then he began walking back home, with the hood of his jacket over his head, cutting in and out of covered areas in the gated community because of the rain. As Trayvon Martin moved among the buildings and through covered passageways, he attracted the attention of a twenty-eight-year-old Hispanic man named George Zimmerman, who was the neighborhood-watch coordinator for the gated community. Mr. Zimmerman called the Sanford Police Department to report what he thought was Trayvon Martin's suspicious behavior: "This guy looks like he's up to no good or he's on drugs or something. It's raining and he's just walking around, looking about. He's just staring and looking at all the houses." At that point, the young man turned toward the truck where Mr. Zimmerman was sitting. "Now he's just staring at me," Zimmerman told the police. "Now he's coming towards me. He's got his hand in his waistband, and he's a black male."

As Trayvon Martin passed Mr. Zimmerman and continued walking toward his father's home, Mr. Zimmerman got out of his truck while still talking to the police on his cell phone and began to follow the young man. "Shit! He's running," Mr. Zimmerman told the police. The police dispatcher asked Zimmerman if he was pursuing Martin. Zimmerman said, "Yes," and the police responded, "We don't need you to do that." At the same time Zimmerman was talking to the police, Trayvon Martin was talking on his own cell phone to a female friend. "A creepy-ass cracker is following me," he told her.

At this point, the details become unclear. A violent encounter between the two men left the unarmed Trayvon Martin dead, shot in the chest with Mr. Zimmerman's nine-millimeter semiautomatic pistol. When the police arrived, Zimmerman said he had been attacked by Martin, and he shot Martin in self-defense. The police noted that Zimmerman's nose was bleeding, that he had cuts on the back of his head, and that the back of his clothes were wet and carried traces of grass trimmings. A witness to the confrontation said he saw Zimmerman lying on the grass, with Martin on top of Zimmerman, punching him. Another pair of witnesses in a nearby apartment said they heard no sounds of a fight until they heard a gunshot. Zimmerman told police that Martin was slamming his head against a concrete sidewalk, but DNA tests found no DNA from Zimmerman's blood on Martin's hands or fingernails. Zimmerman also said that, when Martin saw his gun, Martin tried to grab it, but Zimmerman grabbed it first and fired at Martin. However, none of Martin's fingerprints were found on the gun. Several witnesses called 911, and one of the calls recorded a male voice crying for help in the background. Both Zimmerman's and Martin's parents declared the voice to be that of their son. An expert forensic analysis could not determine whose voice it was because of the poor quality of the recording.

The forensic evidence and witness testimony is inconclusive. Under these circumstances, deciding whether George Zimmerman shot Trayvon Martin in self-defense depends on how jurors interpret the facts. What stories do jurors tell themselves, based on their personal experiences, about what must have happened that rainy night?

To complicate matters further, Florida's Stand Your Ground law openly invites storytelling. George Zimmerman was charged by the state with second-degree murder. Under the Stand Your Ground law, in order to find Mr. Zimmerman not guilty of second-degree murder by virtue of self-defense, the jury had to decide that Trayvon Martin's death resulted from the "justifiable use of deadly force." Judge Debra Nelson instructed the jury as follows:

> In deciding whether George Zimmerman was justified in the use of deadly force, you must judge him by the circumstances by which he was surrounded at the time the force was used. The danger facing George Zimmerman need not have been actual; however, to justify the use of deadly force, the appearance of danger must have been so real that a reasonably cautious and prudent person under the same circumstances would have believed that the danger could be avoided only through the use of that force. Based upon appearances, George Zimmerman must have actually believed that the danger was real. . . . If in your consideration of the issue of self-defense you have a reasonable doubt on the question of whether George Zimmerman was justified in the use of deadly force, you should find George Zimmerman not guilty.[1]

The key words here are that the danger "need not have been actual" and that George Zimmerman "actually believed the danger was real." And the "appearance of danger must have been so real that a reasonably cautious and prudent person under the same circumstances would have believed that the danger could be avoided only through the use of [deadly] force." In other words, the law invited jurors to put themselves in George Zimmerman's shoes and imagine what they would have felt if they themselves had seen the same danger that Mr. Zimmerman thought he saw when he shot Trayvon Martin. The judge also instructed the jurors to "use your common sense in deciding which is the best evidence." In support of this instruction, the judge informed the jurors, "You may rely upon your own conclusion about the witness. A juror may believe or disbelieve all or any part of the evidence of the testimony of any witness."[2]

Given the inconclusive evidence and the judge's charge that a "reasonably cautious and prudent person" would have had to believe the danger to be so real that the use of deadly force was justified in self-defense, which kind of storytellers would you have wanted on the jury if you wished to find George Zimmerman innocent of second-degree murder? And which kind would you want if you wished to find Mr. Zimmerman guilty?

You might be thinking that, in order to find Mr. Zimmerman innocent of second-degree murder, you would want people on the jury who could empathize with him because they had been victims of assault or because they feared assault by strangers. Perhaps you would want people who doubted whether they were strong enough to defend themselves adequately against assault by a stranger or people who had armed themselves in advance against the possibility of assault. You might feel that women are more likely than men to fear assault and to doubt their capacities to defend themselves. You might also suppose that people who were unfamiliar with African American teenagers and who viewed such young men as potential criminals would be sympathetic to Mr. Zimmerman's beliefs and fears and thus imagine that his fears were reasonable under the circumstances and may have justified the use of deadly force in self-defense.

On the other hand, if you wanted to find Mr. Zimmerman guilty of second-degree murder, then you might want people on the jury who were less fearful of assault and who felt more capable of defending themselves, perhaps younger adult males. You might be interested in whether a potential juror felt a sense of control over life events, as opposed to someone who felt victimized by circumstances beyond his or her control. And you might suppose that someone familiar with young African American males and their style of dress would not necessarily view a person with Trayvon Martin's characteristics, clothes, and behavior as a potential criminal.

If you reasoned in accord with either of these paragraphs, then you would be intuitively picking one or another type of potential storyteller as your preferred juror. But confronted with a group of sixty people chosen at random from state voter lists and driver's license holders, how could you identify which potential jurors in the panel might fear assault and believe they should arm themselves in case of harm? Which jurors might feel unfairly victimized by life's circumstances? Which jurors might harbor suspicions of strangers? And which jurors would likely be unfamiliar with the styles and habits of young African American males?

Pretrial Jury Questionnaires

One way to identify jurors who would feel more or less fearful of assault or more or less sympathetic with young African American males is to ask all potential jurors to fill out a pretrial questionnaire. The questionnaire would have dozens of items submitted by each side's attorneys and approved in advance by the judge. Potential jurors would return the questionnaires to the court a day or so before the trial is set to begin. The attorneys for each side, and perhaps their jury consultants, would sit up late at night, combing through every juror's answer to each question, highlighting particularly interesting answers, underlining responses to follow up in court, and scoring each juror for his or her favorability to the prosecution or the defense.

Attorneys often include "pet" questions in pretrial questionnaires that they hope will open a window on jurors' minds. Such questions might include "What bumper stickers do you have on your car?" Or "Name three people you admire most and least." Or "What are your favorite TV shows?" Or "List the last three books you have read." Potential jurors' answers to such questions seldom reveal likely verdicts but are often entertaining. A few years back, I was reviewing the pretrial questionnaire of an older man in Texas who identified the three people in the world he admired least, in the following order, as Bill Clinton, Satan, and Hillary Clinton. On another occasion, I noted that the last two books read by a lady in Georgia were Dolly Parton's autobiography and The Illustrated Children's Bible. Neither of these answers was very useful in trying to predict which verdict that juror might reach in a specific case, but they brightened the late-night hours and reminded me that I was working with real human beings.

Pretrial jury questionnaires usually begin with general questions about a potential juror's demographics, such as gender, ethnicity, education, income, religion, political affiliation, and the like. But such questions seldom predict the verdict a juror will reach in a trial. Sometimes a potential juror's ethnicity or gender may be related to that juror's verdict but usually only when ethnicity or gender are the driving issues in the trial. In the O. J. Simpson murder trial, for example, Simpson's African American race was perhaps the single-most crucial factor in the trial. National opinion surveys showed that a majority of African Americans viewed Mr. Simpson as an innocent victim of racist police officers, who manipulated blood samples to make Mr. Simpson appear guilty. The same opinion surveys showed that most white Americans viewed Mr. Simpson as clearly guilty of murdering his wife and her friend.

As in the O. J. Simpson case, in the Zimmerman trial, African American jurors might have viewed George Zimmerman's claim of self-defense differently than would white jurors. In most cases though, when ethnicity or gender appear to predict a juror's verdict, it is usually because a juror's ethnicity or gender stand in for other factors, such as a feeling of powerlessness or a sense of victimization or a distrust of powerful corporations. According to psychological research, the characteristics that best predict a juror's verdict in a trial are not general demographics but case-specific attitudes and experiences.[3] Jurors' relevant attitudes and life experiences provide the lenses through which they evaluate the evidence. For example, in an assault and murder case, such as the Zimmerman trial, a juror's case-specific attitudes might involve fears of being assaulted, worry over not being able to protect oneself walking alone at night, and even fears of unfamiliar strangers. Relevant experiences could include being a victim of a robbery or mugging, living in a gated community, or owning a gun in order to protect oneself.

In the Zimmerman trial, jury selection began with about five hundred people receiving a summons to report for jury duty. Everyone in the pool filled out an extensive questionnaire about his or her background, experience with crime and guns, and views on numerous social issues. A number of people were quickly excused for hardship or because they already knew too much about the case. The judge and the attorneys on both sides then spent eight days winnowing the pool further. Some people were excused because they admitted they had already made up their minds about who should win the trial. Others were excused because they had taken part in demonstrations demanding that Mr. Zimmerman be brought to trial or because they supported the demonstrations. Finally, forty potential jurors, twenty-six females and fourteen males, went through a second round of one-on-one questions from the judge and the attorneys. The entire process took almost nine days.

The questionnaire that jurors filled out was not made public, but the questions asked by each side's attorneys during the oral voir dire suggest the kinds of issues that must have been included in the questionnaire. According to a legal blogger who attended every day of voir dire, the prosecution who brought the case against Mr. Zimmerman asked potential jurors whether they had ever been arrested, been a victim of a crime, believed crime was a problem in their community, knew if their community had a neighborhood-watch program, and believed if it was right to take the law into their own hands. The prosecution then went on to ask prospective jurors if they owned any guns and if their family and friends owned any guns.[4]

Fourteen prospective jurors revealed that they had been victims of a crime. One said she had been robbed under circumstances very similar to Mr. Zimmerman's testimony. "It's always on my mind," she said. Another stated that her workplace had been robbed twice at gunpoint and the police who responded were "snide" and "scared her more than the robber." Ten prospective jurors lived in communities with neighborhood-watch programs, and one said her husband was a block captain in such a program. Eleven potential jurors reported that they owned guns, and one said he was a firearms instructor. Twelve other panel members said someone in their family owned a gun. One juror who promised the judge that he could be fair and impartial had previously posted a rant against the Sanford Police Department on a social media site. Some of these jurors were excused for cause, which means that the judge agreed that the jurors would have a hard time being impartial. By the time Zimmerman's own attorneys began their questioning of the jurors, not many questions were left to be answered. The defense voir dire went quickly.

Picking the Zimmerman Jury

Under Florida law, each side's attorneys in the Zimmerman trial could exercise ten peremptory strikes. This means that each side could strike up to ten potential jurors from the forty-person pool without stating a cause, so long as the jurors were not struck merely because of their gender or ethnicity. The prosecution struck only six jurors, although two of the six strikes were rejected by the judge when the defense objected. One of the six was struck because she mentioned that Trayvon Martin had been expelled from school. The defense struck just two jurors, one of whom was struck because her pastor had written a letter in support of Trayvon Martin.

Why, you might ask, wouldn't each side use all ten of its peremptory strikes to remove jurors with whom it might feel uncomfortable? The reason is that removing jurors with peremptory strikes is something of a chess game. When you strike a juror, the stricken juror is replaced with another juror from the panel. Sometimes, the juror who replaces the stricken juror may present more of a problem than the juror who was struck. Also, attorneys frequently try to outguess the opposing side's strikes: "If we strike the older white lady with a policeman son, who will they strike?" For these reasons, attorneys frequently find it less of a gamble to accept a jury without using all available peremptory strikes than to use up all possible strikes and take their chances on who replaces a stricken juror.

When each side's attorneys finished striking jurors in the Zimmerman trial, the final six-person jury contained five white women and one Hispanic woman:

- **Juror 1** was a middle-aged, white woman who lived in a community with a neighborhood-watch program, had reported vandalism to the watch program, owned rental property, had family members who own guns, and said she "rescues a lot of pets."
- **Juror 2** was a middle-aged, white woman who described the local demonstrations demanding that Mr. Zimmerman be brought to trial as

"rioting," formerly held a concealed weapons permit, and was married to a man who had a concealed weapons permit.

- **Juror 3** was a retired, unmarried, white woman with no children who knew a lot about the case, thought Mr. Zimmerman may have done nothing wrong because he was on neighborhood watch but that he should have waited when the police told him not to pursue Mr. Martin, and said she "wasn't rigid in her thinking."
- **Juror 4** was a younger, white mother of two adolescent children who forbade her kids from going out alone at night; attended church regularly; volunteered at her kids' school; and had visited a shooting range with her husband, who owned many guns.
- **Juror 5** was a sixty-ish married, white mother of a twenty-eight-year-old son who loved football, had been a victim of crime, and said she had worked as a safety officer for twenty-five years.
- **Juror 6** was a married, Hispanic mother of eight children who was a night-shift nurse on an Alzheimer's ward, had been a resident of Chicago when Trayvon Martin was killed, and knew nothing about the case except that some of her friends and family were on the side of the child.
- The **alternate jurors** were two women and two men. They sat through the case but did not deliberate.

If you're curious about why no African Americans were on the jury, part of the answer is that, in Seminole County, Florida, where the trial was held, only about 11 percent of the population is black. Furthermore, the pretrial jury questionnaire winnowed out a number of African Americans because of their answers to questions about whether they attended or supported any demonstrations calling for Mr. Zimmerman to be brought to trial for killing Trayvon Martin. The fewer African Americans in the jury pool, the less likely are black defendants to be found not guilty (and in this this instance, Trayvon Martin was turned into a defendant because Mr. Zimmerman argued that Martin was the attacker).[5]

Now, you may be thinking, with the benefit of hindsight, "It's so obvious how a group of six women, only one of whom was not white, would view the evidence and find in favor of Mr. Zimmerman." But it wasn't necessarily obvious to attorneys at the time. The *Miami Herald* quoted one local attorney as saying, "Females bring in the parental, maternal instinct of being sympathetic toward the victim, who was a young kid in high school."[6] Another local attorney was quoted as saying the exact opposite: "Women may side with Zimmerman over issues of self-defense." A jury consultant hired by

Zimmerman's attorneys stated in USA Today, "Women would relate to Zimmerman's story better than men and would understand the position Zimmerman found himself in on the night of the shooting."[7]

I side with the jury consultant, who was essentially saying that women would be more likely to tell a story about the facts of that evening that resembled Mr. Zimmerman's own story. From this perspective, women would be more likely than men to fear assault in the dark; women would be more likely to protect themselves from assault by carrying on their person some form of self-defense; women might be more alarmed by allegations of being attacked by an unfamiliar young man; and the five white women could have imagined a greater threat posed by a young black male wearing a hoodie on a dark rainy night, who appeared to be running between condos in a gated community. Add that three of the women had family members who owned guns, two were familiar with neighborhood-watch programs, and another described herself as a safety officer who had been a crime victim, and you might predict a slam-dunk verdict for the defense.

Juror's Voir Dire Responses and Their Verdicts

After a day and a half of deliberations, the six-woman jury returned a verdict in favor of George Zimmerman. A few days later, two of the women discussed the deliberations on television news programs, and four others released a joint statement to the press. These public comments revealed that initially the jury was divided, with three jurors finding Zimmerman guilty, and three finding him not guilty. Deliberations started late in the afternoon on Friday, July 14. By Saturday afternoon, the three not-guilty jurors had convinced two of the three guilty jurors to join them in a not-guilty verdict. This left one holdout, the Hispanic mother of eight children, whose friends favored the "child." After nine hours of deliberations, this woman was finally persuaded that George Zimmerman was not guilty of manslaughter in the death of Trayvon Martin.

How the six jurors came to this view is reflected in public comments of juror 2, a woman who formerly owned a concealed weapons permit and described the demonstrations demanding that Mr. Zimmerman be brought to trial as "riots." Three days after the verdict, this juror was interviewed by Anderson Cooper on CNN.[8] She said she had "no doubt" that Mr. Zimmerman "feared for his life." "I think George Zimmerman is a man whose heart was in the right place," she said, "but just got so displaced by the vandalism in the neighborhoods, and wanting to catch these people so badly, that he went above and beyond what he really should have done." She went on, "Anybody would think anybody walking down the road, stopping and turning and looking, if that's exactly what happened, is suspicious. . . . I think George got in a little bit too deep, which he shouldn't have been there. But Trayvon decided that he wasn't going to let him scare him . . . and I think Trayvon got mad and attacked him." Such comments represent a classic example of a juror telling a story, with personal embellishments, in order to make sense of the facts.

After juror 2 appeared on CNN, four other jurors released a statement saying that juror 2's opinion did not represent their own views. A week later, on ABC's *Good Morning America*, the minority woman who had been the lone holdout made it clear how jurors came to their verdicts in an interview: "I was the juror who was going to give them a hung jury." "I fought to the end," she declared, seemingly revealing that she held an alternative story of what happened. But she changed her mind, she explained, because "if you have no proof that he killed him intentionally, you can't say he's guilty." Even though this juror admitted on television that she thought George Zimmerman "got away with murder," she defended her verdict by noting that the evidence "did not prove murder."[9]

The judge's instructions allowed jurors to acquit Mr. Zimmerman of the charge of manslaughter if the killing "was committed by accident or misfortune . . . without any unlawful intent [or] upon sudden and sufficient provocation."[10] By inferring no unlawful intent, as juror 2 stated, the jury had to find George Zimmerman not guilty of manslaughter. In other words, the six-woman jury, including a minority woman, accepted Zimmerman's story that he acted in self-defense when he shot Trayvon Martin. Would a jury composed of six men or six African Americans or six individuals who disapproved of carrying a concealed weapon or six people who had no experience with neighborhood-watch programs have reached the same verdict? In my view, the story model of jury decision making would say probably not.

Chapter Summary

Jury selection is about selecting storytellers. Jurors' likely stories about the facts of a case can be predicted by their responses to carefully crafted voir dire questions. The voir dire questions must assess jurors' case-specific attitudes and behaviors—their relevant life experiences, not general demographic characteristics, which have little predictive value. And the best way to assess jurors' case-specific experiences and attitudes is through a detailed written questionnaire that jurors fill out before a trial begins.

In the George Zimmerman trial, a juror's verdict could have been understood and predicted in advance by voir dire questions that assessed the juror's experiences and attitudes with crime, guns, neighborhood-watch committees, threats to safety, and unfamiliarity with African American teenage males. Also, Florida's Stand Your Ground law invited jurors to rely on their personal experiences in order to imagine whether George Zimmerman feared for his life when he shot Trayvon Martin. In other words, jurors were encouraged to tell stories in order to understand the evidence.

In the next chapter, let's turn from a criminal trial to a civil trial and look at the types of people who tend to favor the plaintiff or the defense in a product-liability lawsuit and how they might be identified.

CHAPTER SIX

Jury Selection in a
Product-Liability Lawsuit

If a juror's fear of assault explains the kind of story a juror will tell about the evidence in a self-defense murder trial, then which characteristics explain the type of story a juror will tell in a civil case, dealing with an allegedly defective product, for example? In such cases, a person files a lawsuit against a manufacturer because the person believes he or she has been injured by a product made and sold by the manufacturer. The purpose of the lawsuit is to request compensation for the injury that the person believes the product caused and, under certain circumstances, to punish the manufacturer for knowingly making an unsafe product. If you were an attorney representing a person who filed such a lawsuit against a manufacturer, then which sort of jurors—or storytellers—would you want to see in the jury box to make sure they were not biased against your client? On the other hand, if you were an attorney representing the manufacturer, then which kind of storytellers would you want to see in the box who would not be biased against manufacturers or big corporations?

As a jury consultant, I have worked on a great many product-liability lawsuits. Many involved auto manufacturers being sued by a person or group of persons who claimed that some defect in the manufacturer's vehicle caused them to suffer serious injury, such as the power-window switch in chapter 1. Others include pharmaceutical companies whose drugs allegedly caused unexpected harmful side effects, home appliance makers whose stoves or washers or coffee makers were said to have caused house fires, medical device manufacturers whose products seemingly failed to work as designed, industrial supply companies whose components allegedly malfunctioned and led to explosions, and chemical companies whose liquids or gases allegedly polluted the air we breathe and the water we drink. This partial listing of cases involving alleged defects in manufactured products may make you view the world as a toxic environment. Safety threats and unknown perils abound. Hazards lurk behind every household device. Catastrophic harm can be unleashed with the flip of a switch. Entering a vehicle could lead to a disastrous accident.

Whether the world is really so toxic, so threatening, so full of hazards or not depends in large part on how people appraise risks. According to common jury instructions, a product is "unreasonably dangerous because of its design if it fails to perform as safely as an ordinary consumer would expect when used as intended or in a manner reasonably foreseeable by the manufacturer." A product may also be found "unreasonably dangerous because of inadequate instructions or warnings when the foreseeable risks of harm posed by the product could have been reduced or avoided by the provision of reasonable instructions or warnings and the omission of the instructions or warnings renders the product not reasonably safe." A related jury instruction explains that a manufacturer may be found "negligent" if the manufacturer "fails to use reasonable care" in making and marketing the vehicle. *Reasonable care* is defined as "that degree of care which a reasonably careful person would use under like circumstances."

As you may have realized, a juror's task in a typical product-liability lawsuit is not vastly different from the jurors' task in the Trayvon Martin murder trial. Just as a juror in the Zimmerman trial had to decide if Mr. Zimmerman reasonably feared grievous bodily harm when he shot Trayvon Martin, a juror in a product-liability trial has to decide if a manufacturer used reasonable care in designing a vehicle for an ordinary consumer to use in a foreseeable manner. But what is "reasonable"? Who is an "ordinary consumer"? Which types of vehicle uses are "reasonably foreseeable"? Which types of instructions and warnings are "adequate"? And how might jurors disagree on the meaning of these concepts? In order to make these questions more concrete, let's look at the details of a typical case on which my firm ran a mock trial.

A few years ago, three high school boys in the spring of their senior year decided to take a road trip to see an athletic event. They spent Friday night at one boy's house and left for their trip after breakfast the next morning in a late-model sport utility vehicle owned by the mother of one of the boys. Their plan was to watch the athletic event, stay in a hotel Saturday night, and return home on Sunday morning. Along the way, they changed their minds and decided that, instead of going to the sports event, they would visit some friends who had graduated from their school the year before and were freshmen at a nearby university. The boys found their friends, went to a party Saturday night, hung out, watched a video, and in the early hours of

Sunday morning decided not to check into a hotel but to drive several hours back home.

The boy who was least sleepy started driving home between 3:00 and 4:00 a.m. with his seat belt fastened. A second boy climbed into the back seat, lay down across the seat, and did not fasten his seat belt. The third boy took the front passenger's seat, buckled his seat belt, and reclined the seat as far as it would go so he could sleep. The boys were driving on a four-lane interstate highway. After a couple hours, the driver said he was feeling sleepy, so he woke up the boy in the back seat and asked him to take the wheel. Two hours later, at around 8:15 Sunday morning, the boy who was driving said that he fell asleep at the wheel. He woke up when he heard the sound of the vehicle's tires passing over the highway's rumble strips, those little grooves in the shoulder of a freeway that let you know when you're running off the road. The sport utility vehicle was traveling at seventy to eighty miles per hour when it veered off the shoulder and started down a grassy slope in the median between the two sides of the interstate. The driver quickly turned the steering wheel to get the vehicle back on the highway, which caused it to slide diagonally down the shoulder, until the friction of the tires on the roadway caused the vehicle to trip and roll over. Impact marks showed that the vehicle rolled five and a quarter times before it came to rest, more than a hundred feet down the highway. The boy who was driving survived the accident with a broken arm. The boy lying down in the back seat survived as well. But the boy in the front passenger's seat, who was wearing his seat belt loosely fastened, with his seat fully reclined, was thrown out of the vehicle, hurled fifty feet, and killed.

The family of the deceased boy sued the manufacturer of the vehicle, claiming that the vehicle had three defects: First, the boy's family said that the vehicle had handling problems, which made it too easy for a sharp twist on the steering wheel to cause an overcorrection and send the vehicle into a sideways slide down the road. Second, his family said that the vehicle was top heavy because it was too high and too narrow, which made it easy to tip over once it started sliding down the road. And third, they said that the vehicle lacked adequate warnings to passengers not to recline the seat too far because that would make the seat belt less effective. So, even though the driver fell asleep and the vehicle drove onto the edge of the median, the family believed that their son would still be alive if the vehicle had not begun sliding sideways down the road, tipped over at a high speed, rolled over, and allowed their belted son to be ejected from his reclined front passenger seat. The manufacturer replied that a sports utility vehicle has a higher center of gravity than a passenger car because it was designed to travel off road, that the vehicle handled normally but the driver had jerked the steering wheel so sharply that he put the vehicle into a slide, and the owner's manual warned about not reclining the seats too far because it made the seat belts less effective.

Which type of jurors would be the least biased against the boy's family, and which type would be the least biased against the manufacturer? You already know how the jury-selection process unfolds. The goal is to identify people who come to the courtroom with attitudes and life experiences that lead them to be suspicious and tell unflattering stories about one side or the other. A juror who is potentially biased against the teenage boys in this case might have had an accident on the highway when a teenage male driver ran into the juror's car or a family member's car. Maybe someone was seriously injured. Perhaps the juror was in a serious accident as a young person and regretfully blames it on his own lack of caution. Or a juror views teenage males as impulsive, reckless risk takers. "Who knows what the boys drank at that party?" a juror might ask. Or "I would never drive on the highway after being up all night," another might think. Such views could easily cause a juror to be less interested in the defect allegations against the manufacturer than in the boys' own responsibility for the accident and the ejection of the passenger whose seat was fully reclined.

On the other side, a juror might arrive at the courtroom with negative views about the sport utility vehicle's manufacturer. Perhaps the juror had a bad experience with one of the manufacturer's dealers or had driven a vehicle with a higher center of gravity and thought it was hard to control or simply distrusted corporations in general. Being the type of person who chronically worries about accidents and harm or who imagines an inability to protect oneself against harm could also lead to sympathizing with the plaintiff and finding against the manufacturer.

Once again, a juror's life experience and attitudes can easily lead one juror to tell a very different story about the evidence in a case than another juror would tell. For example, just as women jurors in the Zimmerman trial may have been more afraid of a nighttime assault than males or residents of communities with neighborhood-watch programs may have been more sympathetic with Mr. Zimmerman than people who lived in communities without volunteer guards or gun owners may have been more accepting of Mr. Zimmerman's armed self-defense than people who didn't own guns, certain jurors in an automotive-design case would be more likely to find a vehicle "unreasonably dangerous." It's not necessarily a question of one group of jurors being right and another being wrong. It's a question of the facts being viewed differently by different people.

Characteristics of Plaintiff and Defense Jurors in Product-Liability Lawsuits

As a jury consultant, I have run many research exercises that were designed to identify the types of people who tend to favor plaintiffs or defendants in civil lawsuits. Each of these exercises involved from fifty to several hundred paid mock jurors and lasted from an afternoon to two or three days. As part of the research, each juror answered some two hundred questions in a written questionnaire about themselves, their demographic characteristics, their interests and lifestyles, and their attitudes toward issues related to the case. Then they answered another two hundred or so questions about their views of the evidence in each side's case. This allowed us to perform complicated statistical analyses that related a juror's characteristics and attitudes to a juror's verdict. Armed with these analyses, we were able to go a long way toward explaining the types of people who favor plaintiffs and defense in product-liability lawsuits, such as this rollover accident.

First, let's consider whether a juror's ethnicity and gender relate to a juror's verdict because it's an old debate among lawyers. Many lawyers would swear that a juror's gender and ethnicity combine to influence a juror's verdict. For example, lawyers representing corporate defendants, such as the auto manufacturer in this example, tend to favor white males, preferably well off, who have secured a comfortable niche in society. Such jurors are less likely to be suspicious of big corporations, the common wisdom holds.

In contrast, lawyers who represent plaintiffs, like the family of the boy who was killed in the rollover accident, tend to favor females and minorities. They are more vulnerable and more likely to desire protection from harm, conventional wisdom maintains. The prevalence of such beliefs is why courts have ruled that lawyers cannot use a peremptory strike to remove a juror from the panel merely because of a juror's ethnicity or gender. If a lawyer defending an auto company uses too many of the available peremptory strikes to remove minority females from the jury, then the attorney has to show that the minority female is being struck for reasons other than the fact that she is African American or Hispanic and female. Likewise, if an attorney for an injured plaintiff uses too many strikes to remove white males from the jury, then the attorney must convince the judge that the men are not being struck simply because they are white and male.

As it happens, people of different ethnicities and genders often hold quite different attitudes about corporations, for example, and about injured plaintiffs in lawsuits. But that is not because of their ethnicity or gender; rather it's because of the life experiences and resulting attitudes that go along with being African American and female as opposed to being white and male. Or being Hispanic. Or being Asian. Let me repeat, in order to remove any hint of racism or sexism: It's not skin color and genitalia that lead to different appraisals of risky or safe products; it's the life experiences that are accumulated by people of different races and genders.

Two Studies of Juror Demographics and Attitudes as Predictors of Verdict

A few years ago, a young man named Sean Overland was enrolled as a graduate student in political science at the University of California at Los Angeles; at the same time, he worked as an employee for the jury research firm where I was a partner. Sean needed a dissertation topic, and our firm had years of questionnaire data gathered in countless mock trials, conducted in all regions of the United States, using mock jurors who were carefully recruited to match actual jury panels. The data cried out for analysis, and Sean had spent several years learning advanced statistical techniques that perfectly matched our data. The project became Sean's dissertation, which was published as a book, *The Juror Factor: Race and Gender in America's Civil Courts.*[1]

Sean's goal in his study was to determine how important a juror's race and gender were in predicting a juror's verdict. He started with a sample of more than 2,500 subjects from our data pool and focused on three types of mock trials: those involving defective-design allegations against auto manufacturers, those involving claims against prescription drugmakers, and those involving accounting malpractice charges. In other words, cases involving cars, drugs, and high finance. At the most basic level, Sean found that, when he combined all the auto cases, 66 percent of African American jurors found for the plaintiff in these mock trials, while only 31 percent of white jurors found for the plaintiff. Women were also more likely to find for the plaintiff. Across all of the cases involving drugmakers, 64 percent of African American jurors found for the plaintiff, while white jurors roughly split about 50–50 between the plaintiff and defendant. Once again, women tended to favor the plaintiff. And across all accounting cases, African American jurors split about 50–50 in favor of plaintiff or defendant, while almost two-thirds of the white jurors favored the accounting firms. In other words, a majority of African American jurors favored the plaintiff in the auto and drug cases, when an individual was personally injured by the product, while they split about 50–50 in the financial cases, which tended to be between two corporations or between a group of shareholders and a corporation. In contrast, white jurors either favored the corporations or split their verdict between the plaintiff and defendant.

What accounts for these differences between the views of African American jurors and white jurors and between women and men? Another way of asking this question is, Which characteristics, attitudes, and beliefs are so closely associated with a juror's race and gender that they explain why race and gender seem to have such a strong effect on the verdict? To answer this question, Sean used a complicated statistical technique called logistic regression. With this technique, he found that certain types of attitudes are more likely to be held by African Americans and women than by whites and men. These attitudes included a juror's political ideology: African Americans and women were more likely to describe themselves as liberal than middle of the road or conservative. A second attitude was a juror's feelings about big business: African Americans and women were more likely than whites and men to be skeptical of the goals, practices, and ethics of big business and believed business should be more strongly regulated. A third attitude had to do with a juror's views about lawsuits, with African Americans and women more likely to approve of lawsuits and to deny that damage awards in lawsuits were too high, compared to whites and men.

But while a juror's political philosophy, attitudes toward big business, and beliefs about lawsuits went a long way toward explaining a juror's verdict, these attitudes couldn't entirely account for why African Americans and women tended to favor plaintiffs in certain types of product-liability lawsuits. What else could explain why African Americans particularly and women to a lesser extent seem to favor injured plaintiffs over corporations? As Sean states in his book, "The most likely explanation for the remaining difference between jurors of different races is that there are attitudes and beliefs not included in these models that affect verdict."[2] In other words, if Sean's model had included a greater variety of attitudes, then the seeming effect of ethnicity and gender would likely vanish altogether. It would be the worldviews often associated with a jurors' ethnicity and gender that predict a juror's verdict, not the mere fact of a juror's skin color and genitalia.

To test this idea, we decided to comb through ten years of data gathered in hundreds of mock trials conducted by our jury research firm. Our research director, Eric Gober, followed Sean's model, sorting the data into types of cases, such as automotive cases, pharmaceutical cases, accounting cases, contract disputes, consumer products, and the like. For simplicity's sake, let's look at just one category of cases, those involving allegations of defective design against automakers. Over the ten-year period of our study, we conducted twenty-nine different mock trials in which a plaintiff or group of plaintiffs sued various automakers. The twenty-nine mock trials included nearly four thousand subjects. We divided the sample into those mock jurors who favored the plaintiffs and those who favored the defendant at the end of the trials. Then we performed the same logistic regression analysis that Sean Overland had performed, but we added in many more types of attitudes. With this much larger sample of subjects, we found that the following nine clusters of attitudes were statistically important in predicting a juror's verdict for the plaintiff or the defense in a case that involved automakers:

1. Whether a juror has been in accidents or is disabled
2. How much a juror worries about harm and sickness
3. How hard a juror works to avoid potentially dangerous risks
4. Whether a juror believes that potentially harmful products can be used safely
5. Whether a juror believes that he or she is capable of protecting himself or herself from harm
6. How suspicious a juror is of big business
7. Whether a juror believes that corporations need stronger regulations to protect workers and consumers from harm
8. Whether a juror believes that lawsuits are an effective means of resolving disputes
9. Whether a juror believes that lawsuits against corporations and big business are usually justified

When we included these additional attitudes and characteristics in our statistical analysis, the effects of a juror's ethnicity and gender vanished. Ethnicity and gender only appear to determine a juror's verdict because they are so highly correlated with a cluster of attitudes about fear and worry and suspicion and self-protection. Simply put, jurors who favored the plaintiffs in these lawsuits were significantly more likely than jurors who favored the automakers to have had accidents and injuries in the past, to worry about harm and sickness, to try to avoid risks, to fear potentially dangerous products, to doubt if they could protect themselves from harm, to distrust big business, to believe that government regulations help protect workers and consumers, and to favor lawsuits against corporations as effective and usually justified.

As you can see, the type of attitudes that influence a juror's verdict in these auto cases are not very different in principle from the type of attitudes that influence a juror's verdict in the Zimmerman trial discussed in chapter 5. In the Zimmerman trial, the six women who acquitted Mr. Zimmerman included two people who had been victims of crimes, three people whose family owned guns to protect themselves, a juror who lived in a neighborhood-watch community and reported violence to the police, and a woman who told her children not to go out at night because it was too dangerous. The jurors' past experiences, fears, and efforts to protect themselves from harm led them to identify with Mr. Zimmerman and find that he acted in self-defense. As the first Zimmerman juror to appear on television said, "Anybody would think anybody walking down the road, stopping and turning and looking, if that's exactly what happened, is suspicious."[3]

In the twenty-nine mock trials that we studied that involved lawsuits against auto manufacturers, jurors who found against automaker defendants also held a fearful, suspicious, self-protective worldview, like the six jurors who found in favor of George Zimmerman. In each type of trial, the jurors' worldviews led them to tell different stories about whether the auto involved in the lawsuit was unreasonably dangerous and designed according to an ordinary standard of care. Put another way, the facts appeared differently to jurors with different backgrounds, experiences, and attitudes.

Jurors Who Award High and Low Damages in a Product-Liability Lawsuit

Before leaving the topic of why different types of jurors perceive risk and harm differently in trials, let's consider the question of punishment or, in the case of a civil trial, monetary damages. After we conducted our in-house analysis of the factors that influenced whether a juror would favor plaintiff or defendant in twenty-nine lawsuits against auto manufacturers, we went on to focus on the factors that influence how much monetary damages a juror who favors the plaintiffs would award to the plaintiffs. That is, which types of people award higher damages and which types award lower damages?

In a typical trial against auto manufacturers, the plaintiff's attorneys usually request two types of monetary damages. As mentioned earlier, the first is compensatory damages to compensate the plaintiff for injuries, suffering, and losses. The second is punitive damages to punish the manufacturer for gross negligence and to send a message to the manufacturer that it should never again release a defective product on the market.

High Compensatory Damages
Among the roughly four thousand mock jurors who took part in the twenty-nine mock trials, nearly nine hundred jurors awarded compensatory damages against the automakers. We conducted another logistic regression analysis

on these nine hundred mock jurors and found that people who awarded high amounts of compensatory damages differed systematically from people who awarded lower amounts of compensatory damages. Those who awarded higher damages tended to have lower incomes, to have suffered more accidents and illnesses, to worry more about risks, to be more fearful of potentially harmful products, to distrust corporations more, to have a greater desire for stronger safety regulations, and to favor more strongly lawsuits against corporations. In the same way that jurors who favored plaintiffs in mock trials against automakers were worriers who feared harm and risk and identified with victims, plaintiff jurors who awarded high compensatory damages were superworriers who were especially afraid of harm and risk.

High Punitive Damages
Likewise, when we narrowed in on the almost seven hundred jurors in our study who awarded punitive damages against manufacturers, we discovered a similar type of worldview. Compared to jurors who awarded lower punitive damages, those who awarded higher punitive damages tended to worry more about illness and risk, to fear potentially harmful products, and to rely more on self-prescribed remedies to protect themselves from harm. These jurors also tended to have lower educations. Jurors who awarded higher punitive damages were similar to those who awarded higher compensatory damages: They were superworriers who were extremely suspicious of corporations.

Implications for Attorneys Selecting
Jurors in Real Trials

Before we leave this chapter, I have a few words for attorneys about how to take maximum advantage of the jury-selection process. Jurors and potential jurors may also find this advice interesting as observers of the high-stakes maneuvers that underlay jury selection. In order to understand better the kinds of stories that a potential juror will likely tell about each side in a lawsuit, and thus to predict more accurately which verdict a juror will likely reach, an attorney should take the following steps:

1. Don't waste valuable time in voir dire reminding jurors to be impartial and trying to make them like you.
2. Try to assess a jurors' attitudes and experiences on specific, case-related issues, not on general values. The more questions—and the more specific questions—an attorney can ask, the better. Jurors' answers to such questions reveal the types of stories they will tell about the case.

3. Try to obtain a pretrial written questionnaire, where specific case-related questions can be asked more easily. Many judges will agree to such questionnaires because they expedite the voir dire process.
4. If a pretrial written questionnaire is not possible, then use the oral voir dire period as an opportunity to probe jurors' case-specific experiences and attitudes. Ask specific questions of the whole panel, and record individual jurors' answers. Then target those jurors whose answers raise concerns with individual follow-up questions.
5. When possible, conduct comprehensive jury research in advance, with large sample sizes, not small-sample focus groups. This reveals the types of questions that best predict verdict as a function of a juror's ethnicity and gender because we know that a juror's ethnicity and gender is accompanied by different clusters of attitudes.

Chapter Summary

Selecting jurors for a civil trial is similar to selecting jurors for a criminal trial. It's about selecting storytellers. Depending on a juror's life experiences, beliefs, and attitudes, he or she will tell different stories about the evidence. Jurors' stories affect their views of the facts. Just as the six women who acquitted George Zimmerman included people whose experiences and attitudes allowed them to put themselves in Mr. Zimmerman's shoes and conclude that he acted in self-defense, so did the jurors who favored plaintiffs in our twenty-nine mock trials against automakers have experiences and attitudes that allowed them to sympathize with the plaintiffs' allegations of unreasonable risk and danger. Compared to defense-oriented jurors, the plaintiff-oriented jurors in our study had been involved in more accidents, worried more about accidents, were more fearful of risk and harm, were more suspicious that auto companies did not try hard to make safe products, felt a greater desire for government safety regulations, were more likely to favor trials against corporations, and were more approving of high damage awards.

In light of such findings, jury selection is an important step in identifying jurors whose likely stories about the evidence will be so biased that they cannot even remotely remain impartial during the trial. Identifying these jurors can be achieved by asking potential jurors specific questions about their experiences and attitudes on issues directly relevant to the trial. Case-specific questions in a written questionnaire are most useful.

In the next chapter, I turn from jury selection, which occurs in an open courtroom, to jury deliberations that take place behind closed doors. I show how jurors' stories about the respective sides in a dispute determine how jurors behave during deliberations.

CHAPTER SEVEN

Jury Deliberations

The Stories Widen

Jury deliberations are one of the most sacred and secret rituals of American democracy. At the end of a trial, when jurors retire to deliberate, a group of average citizens is empowered to decide right or wrong, to determine guilt or innocence, to send criminal defendants to prison or set them free, to levy hundreds of millions of dollars in damages against people or corporations or find them not liable. But very little is known about jury deliberations. Jury deliberations are not recorded or videotaped. No court reporter sits in and transcribes the words jurors say. As a result, no tangible record exists of what goes on in the jury room. This most basic process of democracy is finally an enigma, a black box. "The jury has spoken," we are told, but we have no idea how jurors reach the verdicts they pronounce.

What we do know about juries is that they are a very special kind of group—an extremely unusual group. Unlike groups based on common interests among members, such as family groups, church groups, professional groups, or fraternal groups, members of a typical jury know nothing about each other when they come face to face. Their sole purpose is to come together briefly to perform a task. But a jury's task is more important than the task of almost any other group of which we may become a member. How do twelve strangers form themselves into a functioning group? How do they reveal their sympathies to each other? How do they seek to persuade each other to reach a unanimous or near-unanimous verdict? How do they deal with intense pressures and conflicts within the group? How do they transform individual stories into a group story? Quite simply, how do they find a path to justice?

In this chapter, I explore the many ways in which juries are unique and how this unique nature affects the way they work. Then, in the next chapter,

I provide actual jurors' disclosures about how they deliberated to reach a verdict based on extensive post-trial jury interviews. My goal is to pierce the secrecy that shrouds jury decision making.

Jury Deliberations

Jury deliberation rooms hardly encourage deep philosophical insights about right or wrong. There is nothing of the grandeur suggested by the concept of a hall of justice. The typical jury deliberation room is a blandly functional space, frequently windowless, with linoleum floors and fluorescent lights; an institutional table and chairs; maybe a blackboard for noting bits of evidence; and often a side table for doughnuts, coffee, a pitcher of water, and cups and glasses. Confined to this space for hours, days, or even weeks, jurors are expected to grapple with extremely complex issues, many of which they have never encountered before in their lives. And they are supposed to do so wisely, dispassionately, and with respect for one another.

Selecting a Leader

After entering the jury room, the jurors' first task is to select a leader. The leader, or foreperson, has the serious job of guiding jurors through masses of evidence presented in the testimony of perhaps dozens of witnesses representing opposing sides. The foreperson must interpret the judge's complex instructions and lead jurors through the ponderous legal language of the verdict form. On top of this, the foreperson must solicit the views of shy jurors, keep rowdy jurors under control, and maintain order in a group of up to twelve frequently fractious people, some of whom just want to reach a verdict as quickly as possible and go home.

Despite the daunting tasks required of a jury foreperson, the selection of this key figure is often brief and perfunctory, and there are no guidelines for jurors to follow. Sometimes a person will volunteer. More likely, a juror will throw out someone's name who may have seemed sociable during breaks throughout the trial. Or the title will be conferred on the first person to speak after the jury sits down, with a juror saying something like, "Well, I guess we have to select a leader." "Why not you?" someone will reply. Rarely, an actual nominating process results in two different names being proposed, and a secret ballot will be held.

Usually forepersons tend to share certain characteristics. Based on mock trial results and published post-trial jury interviews, we can say with some conviction that people who are selected to be jury forepersons are likely to be white, male, educated, and extroverted.[1] They are also likely to have seated themselves in more central or more visible places at the jury table, such as at one end of a rectangular table. My firm's post-trial jury interviews confirm these findings. Of twenty-five reports that identified the jury foreperson's demographic characteristics, nineteen elected forepersons were white males. Five were white females, two of whom were elected after a male had been nominated and refused to accept and one of whom volunteered after a male had been elected but realized he had forgotten his reading glasses. One was a Hispanic male.

I was given a chance to confirm these findings a few years ago when a friend was called to jury duty. My friend was a tall, white, male, English professor. He had heard my predictions about the characteristics of jury forepersons, and being a humanities type, he hoped to prove my social-science predictions wrong. On the day before he was to report for jury duty, I told him that, if he was picked as a jury member and wanted to be foreperson, then he should sit at the end of the table, and given his characteristics, he would be elected. This aroused his antipredictability leanings so strongly that he decided to take me on. On his first day of jury duty, wearing a herringbone sport coat, my friend was picked to be on a jury for an assault and battery case. When the jury retired to deliberate, he walked quickly to the jury room and made it a point to sit conspicuously at the end of a rectangular table. Within a few moments after everyone was settled, he was, indeed, elected foreperson.

Becoming a Group

When a jury begins to deliberate, they do not start their task as a collection of random individuals who sit down across a table from each other and begin to speak their minds. The fact is, the individual jurors have already become a special type of group, with far-reaching implications for the verdict they will ultimately reach—or attempt to reach. From the moment they are selected to join a jury to the time they sit down in the jury room, these newly empaneled jurors are subject to a swarm of forces that subtly transform them from individuals into a group. Because of these forces, the jurors become highly vulnerable to a phenomenon called groupthink.[2] Groupthink is a notorious recipe for faulty decision making, where a striving for group unanimity overwhelms an individual's desire to consider objectively alternative courses of action. In other words, the desire to reach a verdict becomes more important than each individual juror's' objective appraisal of the evidence. Consider the following forces that contribute powerfully to groupthink within a jury.[3]

Similarity

As mentioned earlier, the process of voir dire during jury selection tends to weed out people who have extreme opinions about one side or the other in a trial. It also tends to remove the very rich and the very poor because these people often qualify for excuses due to work or child care. It frequently strips the jury of people who are highly educated, outspoken, or have strong personalities because attorneys worry that such people could lead the jury in unpredictable directions and so strike them. And, within certain limitations imposed by the court, jury selection can remove racial minorities who might be seen to sympathize with plaintiffs or victims of harm in a civil case against a company. As a result, the jury that sits down to deliberate over the evidence is typically a fairly homogeneous group, a key factor for groupthink.

Isolation

After a jury is empaneled, the individual jurors are isolated from other individuals in the courtroom and in society. They mingle together in a separate waiting area until the judge is ready for them to be seated in the jury box. They enter the courtroom and depart as a group, with the attorneys and observers rising to their feet to acknowledge their special status. They sometimes wear identifiers, such as lapel pins or name badges. They are instructed not to discuss the case with anyone, including their family members. In high-profile cases, they may be sequestered, where they are assigned rooms in a hotel, perhaps under armed guard, and are forbidden to go home to their families until the trial is over. All of these conditions create a sense of isolation and insulation from society unlike almost any other experience in life.

Cohesiveness

In addition to being insulated from society, jurors spend a lot of time together, waiting, taking breaks, and eating lunches as a group. Because they are instructed not to talk about the case, they gossip and talk about their jobs, families, hobbies, pets, and neighborhoods. They get to know each other and size up one another. Because the process is unfamiliar, they come to rely on each other for cues about how to behave. They are assigned an important responsibility that they are sworn to uphold. And they are given a complicated problem that they must resolve together. Through this process, strangers become friends and colleagues, which makes for strong group cohesiveness and mutual identification.

Stress

All the factors that lead to group similarity, insulation from society, and high cohesiveness make it hard for jurors to disagree with one another and to accept disagreement from fellow jurors. Disagreements are not trivial, either, because the jury's verdict can easily involve prison sentences or even death in criminal cases and huge damages in civil litigation. And the jury is tasked with resolving disagreements in order to achieve a unanimous or, in states where nine or ten of twelve jurors can convict, a nearly unanimous verdict. If you have experienced the stress of disagreeing with a spouse or teenage son or daughter about a fairly minor domestic dispute, then imagine the much greater stress and anxiety experienced by a juror. As I show later, it's not unusual for deliberations to become fraught with shouting, personal verbal attacks, and even threats of violence.

Uncertainty

Because there are no rules for how a jury should go about reaching a verdict, jurors must grope their way toward a solution, often finding that the process is extremely difficult. Not being able to reach a verdict amounts to failure. Being unable to express oneself or unable to persuade another juror to accept one's own perspective or feeling unable to play a useful role in the deliberations can make a juror feel inadequate or publicly shamed. As a result, some people opt out of the discussion altogether or decide simply to see it through until a verdict can be reached.

Unanimity

Finally, the pressure to reach a unanimous or, in some cases, a near-unanimous decision ups the stakes even higher. If the jury complains to the judge that they are deadlocked, then the judge will almost always instruct them to keep deliberating. Judges are reluctant to accept a hung jury. When no end to deliberations appears to be in sight, the pressures to seek accommodation increase dramatically.

Groupthink

Because of these forces that overtly and covertly influence jurors, juries are highly likely to succumb to groupthink. In groupthink, the majority exerts extreme pressure on the minority to join them in a unanimous decision. Individual jurors who hold a minority position often look for reasons to change their minds and join the majority. As jurors in the minority weaken, jurors among the majority marshal further evidence to justify their opinions and overwhelm the minority. Complicated evidence may be glossed over. Alternative outcomes are ignored. Doubts and concerns about nonconforming evidence are suppressed and censored. As jurors holding a minority position typically cave in, one by one, an illusion of unanimity takes over the group. When one or two jurors continue to hold out but the required ten-of-twelve majority has already been reached, the holdouts are rejected and ignored.

They no longer matter. The decision is made. With great relief, the jury informs the judge that a verdict has been reached.

The Process of Deliberating

When a group of jurors—that is, a jury—has selected a foreperson, they formally begin the process of deliberation. Webster's defines *deliberation* as "long and careful thought or discussion in order to make a decision." In practice, this "long and careful discussion" is seldom the case, unless a defiant minority digs in its heels and refuses to join the majority. Then the discussion can be long but not necessarily careful. Several studies of actual juries, including one that surveyed almost 12,000 civil trials, have found that jury deliberations typically last about three hours. More complex evidence can add an hour or two more, while a death-penalty case can add another four hours, on average.[4]

Regardless of the judge's instructions, most jurors do not delay stating their individual verdicts until all the evidence has been carefully considered. In fact, the exact opposite usually happens. According to post-trial jury interviews, including our own, most juries begin deliberations with each individual juror stating where he or she stands on the question of guilt or innocence before the evidence has even been discussed. The alternative is to turn immediately to the verdict form prepared by the court and take a straw vote on the first question, which usually implies guilt or innocence. The average time that passes before jurors state their positions is about twenty minutes, and seldom does it take more than forty minutes before everyone on the jury knows what everyone else thinks.[5] While this sort of haste seems clearly contradictory with the notion that deliberations involve "long and careful" consideration of all the evidence, it's a reasonable way to begin deliberations if we assume that up to 80 percent of jurors will have made up their minds after the opening statements, as mentioned earlier. It is human nature to state your position and see who agrees with you. Not only do most jurors state their positions within the first half-hour of deliberations, but also when the same position is held by a majority of the jury, the majority position will almost always become the verdict that the jury reaches at the end of deliberations. In other words, if a majority reaches a decision within the first half-hour of deliberations, then that will most likely be the final verdict.[6]

Fifty years ago, the founders of jury research, Harry Kalven Jr. and Hans Zeisel, asked jurors in 225 criminal trials to describe the outcome of their first vote during deliberations. The researchers learned that the majority verdict in the first vote became the final verdict 90 percent of the time. "With very few exceptions," said Kalven and Zeisel, "the first ballot decides the outcome of the trial."[7] Numerous other studies involving both criminal and civil trials, mock juries and real juries, have repeatedly confirmed this finding. Very rarely does the minority end up persuading the majority to change its mind.[8]

The Power of the Majority

Why are the initial majorities so powerful in jury trials? To a large extent, it has to do with how groups work and the pressures of groupthink. In the jargon of jury research, these twin processes are called informational influence and normative influence.[9] Let's look at each of these processes in a little more detail. Then, in the next chapter, I provide several examples of informational influence and normative influence drawn from post-trial jury interviews conducted by my own firm.

Informational Influence: "The More You Hear, the More You Believe"

As individual jurors begin to state their positions and their reasons for holding those positions, jurors learn that others either see the case they same way they do or they do not. The more jurors who agree with an individual juror's opinion, the more confirmed each juror feels in holding that opinion. Also, because a group generates more arguments than any single group member, the majority jurors are able to toss out more arguments in favor of the majority position than minority jurors can provide in favor of the minority position. Likewise, fewer arguments attacking the majority position are presented. Consequently, majority jurors become more certain of their positions and less willing to change their minds. Put simply, the more information that supports an individual juror's initial opinion, the more likely the juror will hold to that position—and more firmly—over the course of deliberations.

Groupthink makes the power of informational influence even stronger. When a juror hears that a majority of the jury feels the same way he or she does, the juror tends to suppress doubts and self-censor comments that might question the majority's position or distance the juror from the majority. Evidence that contradicts the majority view is likely to be ignored or dismissed. Some majority jurors become self-appointed "mind guards" and question or refute any statements or evidence that are inconsistent with the majority view. Often, jurors recount vaguely related events from their own lives or their families' and friends' lives that support the majority position, even though jurors have been instructed by the judge to decide the case based solely on the evidence presented. In this way, information and evidence that support the majority position receive much more attention and elaboration than evidence that contradicts this position.

Normative Influence: "The More You Are Pressured, the More You Comply"

The second reason that the views expressed by a majority of jurors early in deliberations usually become the final verdict has to do with normative influence. Normative influence is nothing more than simple conformity pressures that arise in a jury, or any group for that matter, when the people in the majority try to persuade the people in the minority to change their minds and join the majority. Because many people find it uncomfortable and even embarrassing to face a vocal majority and defend their positions against an onslaught, many people will publicly conform, or cave in, to the group pressure, even though privately they never actually change their minds.

To save face and justify such a public cave-in, a juror who changes his or her mind will typically offer a variety of excuses: "I thought about it overnight, and now I can see your position." Or "When you put it that way, I guess I can see what you mean." Expedience also plays a role, as a juror will occasionally admit that he or she switched sides "because I just didn't want to come back tomorrow." Or "I was so exhausted, I couldn't face another day of deliberations, so I joined the majority."

Chapter Summary

Jurors typically begin deliberations by selecting certain types of people to be the foreperson. Jurors then start telling their individual stories of the case before any evidence has been discussed. The pervasive pressure of groupthink allows the majority story to overwhelm the minority story by marshaling more evidence to support the majority, by suppressing evidence that would favor the minority, and by pressuring the minority to join the majority. And because of these processes, the verdict held by the majority of jurors prior to deliberations typically becomes the unanimous or near-unanimous verdict at the close of the trial.

In the following chapter, I provide several examples of deliberations from real trials. I show how real juries select leaders, begin deliberations, experience groupthink, struggle to understand the evidence, and hammer out verdicts. And I explore whether these examples of real trial deliberations even remotely conform to a judge's instructions about how the jury should deliberate.

CHAPTER EIGHT

Jury Deliberations in Real Trials

Because there are almost no studies of actual jury deliberations, the best way to find out what goes on during deliberations is to contact jurors when a trial is over and ask them to describe what happened. In my own consulting firm, we have often been retained to conduct post-trial jury interviews, many of which I have conducted myself. During these interviews, we spend up to two hours on the phone with individual jurors, asking specific questions about how the jury began deliberations: How did they elect a foreperson? How did they discover where each juror stood over the course of deliberations? Did they review the judge's instructions about the law and consult a verdict form provided by the judge? Then we ask how jurors evaluated the evidence: Did they systematically discuss the evidence that was presented, witness by witness? Did they carefully evaluate the credibility of different witnesses' testimony? Could they understand the evidence and testimony? We also ask at which points during the deliberations jurors changed their minds and what influenced them to change their minds? How was the requisite majority achieved in order to reach a verdict? Were the jurors in the minority genuinely persuaded to change their minds by arguments from fellow jurors in the majority, or did they simply cave in out of exhaustion and a desire to go home? Did all jurors understand and agree with the verdict, or did they acquiesce to save face?

Based on the limited psychological research conducted on jury deliberations and on the extensive post-trial juror interviews conducted by our firm, this chapter reveals what happens in the jury room as jurors reach a verdict. We open the black box and find out how fair and just juries really are.

After any trial, there are always some jurors who simply don't want to talk about the case anymore. They sacrificed days or weeks of their lives to perform jury duty, and they want to move on. They are done with it, they say. They have no interest in talking to an interviewer on the phone. However, there are always jurors who deeply need to talk about the trial they sat through and why they and their fellow jurors reached the verdict they reached. Like many people who experience a significant or traumatic event, these jurors need to ventilate, to rehash, and to justify their decisions. They want to make sure that an outsider can understand how and why they arrived at a specific verdict. They are happy to spend a couple of hours recounting who on the jury said what, who stuck to a position no matter what, and who changed his or her mind and why. When you talk to several of these jurors after a trial is over, you can assemble an accurate picture of exactly what went on during deliberations. You come to see which evidence mattered and which didn't; which evidence jurors failed to understand; when jurors threw up their hands and why; how the majority managed to persuade the minority to change their minds; and who simply gave up and shifted their vote to the majority, even when they still thought the majority was wrong. In the following sections, I draw liberally on post-trial jury interviews that I and my colleagues have conducted and that demonstrate the power of informational and normative influences on a jury's verdict.

Two Drug Trials

Drug Trial 1

A few years ago, my firm conducted jury interviews following a high-profile pharmaceutical trial that received a good deal of media attention because it involved a minor celebrity. The plaintiff was a woman who was injected with a cosmetic drug that, she claimed, spread throughout her system and made her sick for two years. After a two-and-a-half-week trial, the twelve-person jury deliberated for three days before reaching a verdict. Deliberations were somewhat protracted because they began on a Wednesday, with jurors evenly split, six to six. The split was apparent at the very beginning of the deliberations when after electing a foreperson, the jurors turned to the verdict form. The first question on the verdict form asked if the plaintiff's injuries were the result of her drug treatment. Half of the jurors believed that the woman got sick on the morning after her drug treatment; therefore, the drug must have been responsible for her illness, they concluded. The other half was convinced that the plaintiff had always been a sickly person, and the drug had nothing to do with any illness she may have experienced after taking the drug.

As soon as the six-to-six split was obvious, one of the prodefense jurors went to a blackboard in the jury room and listed all of the plaintiff's alleged symptoms. The juror then listed other factors that could have caused the symptoms instead of the drug. Before anyone could comment, things became quite ugly. One of the proplaintiff jurors was extremely antagonistic toward the six jurors who supported the drug company. This man said he had suffered an illness similar to the plaintiff's claimed illness and had gone on disability because of it. He maintained that all of the drug company's witnesses had lied, although he could produce no evidence to support this claim. In his view, the company's experts who testified that the drug did not cause the plaintiff's illnesses were part of a "vast conspiracy among drug manufacturers, physicians, and the FDA" (the government agency that regulates drugs).

According to the jurors who were interviewed, this man's persistence and belligerence stalled deliberations. At the end of the first day, the jurors were still split, six to six. On the second day, Thursday, the man became openly abusive to fellow jurors. "Shut up," he would scream at anyone who questioned him, before turning his back on them. Just before lunch, the man became so agitated that he declared he would no longer take part in the deliberations. Then he dramatically stood up, rushed out of the room, and slammed the door. At this point, the jury foreperson wrote a note to the judge, asking that the uncooperative individual be excused and replaced with an alternate. The judge dismissed the jury for the afternoon.

On Friday morning, the third day of deliberations, the judge excused the uncooperative juror and replaced him with one of the alternates. As it happened, the new juror favored the drugmaker, which shifted the initial verdict from a six-to-six standoff to a seven-to-five majority. With the departure of the proplaintiff juror and his replacement by a procompany juror, the picture changed drastically. The seven procompany jurors spent a couple hours attempting to persuade the five proplaintiff jurors that the scientific evidence just didn't support the plaintiff's claim that the drug spread through her system within twenty-four hours after she was injected. The jury then broke for lunch.

After lunch, the jury reconvened, well aware of the fact that it was Friday afternoon and they would have to return to court on Monday if they were unable to reach a verdict within the next few hours. The foreperson suggested that they take another vote on the first question in the verdict form, regarding the drugmaker's responsibility for the plaintiff's illness. This vote revealed that two jurors had changed their minds over lunch: The majority in favor of the drugmaker was now nine to three. Because a three-fourths majority was all that was required, the jury quickly declared a verdict in favor of the drugmaker, informed the judge of their decision, and went home early on Friday afternoon.

What happened after lunch on Friday afternoon, when a seven-to-five majority quickly became a nine-to-three majority and the jury reached a verdict? The two jurors who switched sides simply said they changed their minds over lunch. But it is easy to see the effects of informational and normative influences. On the informational side, the defense jurors all agreed on a clear and simple story. In their view, the plaintiff had suffered from the symptoms she attributed to the drug long before she ever took the drug. Thus, the drug could not have caused her illness. As one of the jurors said, "There wasn't anything wrong with her that wasn't wrong with her before she ever took that drug."

In contrast, the proplaintiff jurors were worried that the drug wasn't absolutely safe, but they had a hard time marshaling scientific evidence in support of this view. The best story they could come up with was that the plaintiff got sick after she took the drug, so the drug must have caused her illness, even though they couldn't explain how the drug caused the illness. This story wasn't strong enough to withstand the simple prodefense story, however. Then the normative forces kicked in. With the proplaintiff jurors now in the minority and the weekend quickly approaching, two of the plaintiff jurors apparently caved in. Because the court only required nine of the twelve jurors to agree in order to declare a verdict, the nine procompany jurors ignored the remaining three proplaintiff jurors and declared a verdict. The simpler story and the growing majority prevailed.

Drug Trial 2
Not long after this drug trial, my firm was hired to interview twelve jurors who sat through an almost identical drug trial but reached a very different conclusion. This second trial involved the same drug, the same claim of illness after injection, and the same warring scientific experts. The difference was the plaintiff. Instead of a woman who came across as a whiny, wannabe celebrity, this second trial involved a female physician, who had a good reputation in a small midwestern city. Even more important, unlike the plaintiff in the first trial, this second plaintiff lacked a history of illnesses similar to the illness that she blamed on the drug. Consequently, the jurors in the second trial were unable to adopt the simple story that any symptoms the plaintiff suffered after she took the drug were the same as the symptoms she suffered before she took the drug. This absence of the "nothing new" story left the jurors vulnerable to the alternative story: that the woman got sick the day after she took the drug, so the drug must have caused her illness.

After the jurors entered the jury room on the first afternoon of deliberations, they elected a foreperson. Then they went around the table, and each person stated his or her verdict. This time the majority was eight in favor of the plaintiff and four in favor of the drug company. If just one person would switch sides, then the jury could reach the required nine-to-three majority in order to declare a verdict in favor of the plaintiff. What do you think happened next?

As in the previous trial, deliberations quickly turned ugly. The eight-to-four deadlock persisted from early afternoon to 9:00 that evening. According to the foreperson, "People were ready to fight. Some turned their backs on the table. About half said they were going home and wouldn't come back." "There were a lot of nice people on the jury," according to the foreperson, "but most of them were completely lost." A female juror said, "A lot of the jurors got overloaded with all the science and just stopped hearing it because most of it wasn't in layman's terms." A male juror echoed the same sentiments: "I didn't understand it. I'm not Einstein. I'm as blue collar as you can get." A second male juror added, "Most people just didn't understand the case." Even the foreperson conceded, "I have no idea what hurt the woman. I'm not a doctor." A female juror summed it up this way: "The plaintiff didn't put on much of a science case, and the company's case was hard to understand." As a result, she noted, the science "just didn't matter to most jurors." The foreperson added, "Most jurors thought the doctor was clearly sick and deserved something." As one of the jurors told us, this conclusion was just "commonsense reasoning."

Without hearing an understandable science case about how and why the drug either did or did not cause the doctor's illness, and feeling sympathetic with the plaintiff, eight of the jurors held fast to the story that the doctor got sick after she took the drug, so the drug must have caused her sickness. In other words, rather than deliberating over the evidence for and against the drug's hazards, most jurors adamantly dug in their heels. At dinnertime on the first day of deliberations, the jury sent a note to the judge stating that they were deadlocked. The judge sent back a message to keep working. Late that evening, the jurors went home exhausted.

On the second morning of deliberations, the foreperson attempted to break the logjam with a new tactic. Instead of trying to answer the first question on the verdict form, which asked if the drug company was responsible for plaintiff's illness, the foreperson suggested that the jury move onto the second question on the verdict form. The second question asked if the drug company was negligent in its warnings, advertisements, or promotion of the drug. The foreperson proposed that the jury could find the manufacturer negligent but not necessarily responsible or liable for the plaintiff's illness. As the foreperson put it, the drug wasn't really a "bad product; it was only bad if you took too much." This compromise allowed the jury to award compensatory damages to the plaintiff, thus covering her medical expenses and lost income, without having to award punitive damages against the company for its liability in making and marketing the drug. The foreperson admitted on the phone during his interview that this compromise "didn't make sense to him. But when everything was going to hell in a handbag, this was the best I could do. The verdict was a compromise I could live with, but half of the jurors could give a shit."

With this compromise on the table, two of the prodefense jurors immediately switched sides and announced that they would join the plaintiff's majority in finding the drug manufacturer negligent but not liable for the plaintiff's illness. The new majority then decided to award the plaintiff $15 million in compensatory damages, while awarding zero punitive damages. One of the jurors who switched sides declared that "$15 million dollars was just a drop in the bucket" to the drugmaker. The foreperson added that "most of the jurors just wanted to go home and not have to return to discuss punitive damages." Another juror told us she voted for the compromise because "she wasn't coming back another day." A third juror admitted that "most people didn't want to come back for more days, and everybody said they were dead set in their positions, so each side found a compromise that would allow them to go home."

This case may seem like a sad commentary on the jury system, with tired and frustrated jurors agreeing to a paradoxical compromise in order to go home after one and a half days of deliberations. Yet it demonstrates how a commonsense story (i.e., the plaintiff got sick a day after taking the drug) can trump days of scientific testimony when the science is unclear and when there is no simple alternative-cause story, such as a preexisting condition. It also suggests that half of the four jurors in the minority would accept any face-saving compromise in order to join the majority and reach a verdict. And it shows once again that the majority at the beginning of deliberations determines the verdict at the conclusion of deliberations.

Three Auto-Accident Trials

The same mix of informational influences, normative influences, and just plain expediency can be seen in three similar auto-accident trials. These trials involved different makes of sport utility vehicles, each of which rolled over at a high speed after the driver made an abrupt steering maneuver.

In each accident, one or more of the occupants was seriously injured. In all three trials, the jury found in favor of the automakers. And in each trial, an initial majority verdict ultimately became the jury's final verdict. In all three cases, my firm conducted lengthy post-trial jury interviews with the actual trial jurors.

Auto Trial 1

A woman was driving a high-end sports utility vehicle at highway speed when another vehicle veered into her path. As she turned her steering wheel to avoid the other vehicle, hers went into a skid and rolled over. During the rollover, the vehicle's roof crushed partly into the passenger compartment and injured the driver. The driver sued the automaker, claiming her vehicle had a design defect that allowed her to be injured in the rollover accident.

Deliberations begin with the jury electing a foreperson. Then the twelve-person jury turned to the first question on the verdict form, which asked if the manufacturer was responsible for the woman's injuries. Each juror stated his or her position on that question, which yielded an initial vote of five believing the vehicle was defective and seven believing it was not. One juror we interviewed said that two plaintiff jurors did not seem to decide on the basis of the evidence but on other factors. One of these jurors had recently suffered a similar injury and said she "knew what the plaintiff was going through." The other was suspicious of corporations and told her fellow jurors that "people and corporations with money have a responsibility to those who do not." She declared that she was in favor of "wealth redistribution." A third proplaintiff juror was an engineer who was convinced that the vehicle that rolled over "could have been more safely designed." In response to his arguments, the promanufacturer jurors argued that the vehicle "passed government safety tests" and that "any vehicle would have had a hard time withstanding the forces of the high-speed rollover." This discussion went on for most of the second day of deliberations.

On the morning of the third day, one of the proplaintiff jurors announced that he had switched sides and now favored the automaker. He said that he "hadn't really understood the evidence until the defense jurors explained it." He also said that originally he had been "swayed by sympathy for the injured plaintiff." When this man switched sides, the vote then stood at four favoring the plaintiff and eight supporting the manufacturer. Only one more prodefense vote was needed to obtain a nine-to-three majority and declare a verdict in favor of the manufacturer. But the four proplaintiff jurors were fixed in their opinions and wouldn't budge. Was the jury about to hang?

As in one of the earlier drug cases, when the jury appeared unable to reach a verdict on the first question on the verdict form, the foreperson suggested that they move onto the second question, having to do with the auto manufacturer's negligence. During discussion of this question, one plaintiff juror became convinced that the plaintiff was not injured when the vehicle's roof crushed partially into the passenger compartment but at another point during the rollover. Consequently, this juror said he changed his mind and now favored the defense, which gave the defense jurors the nine-vote majority they needed in order to declare a verdict. But instead of declaring a verdict and going home, the defense jurors decided to sleep on it and come back in the morning. The next morning, on day 4 of deliberations, the jury took a final vote and found the nine-vote majority in favor of the manufacturer still held. They declared a verdict in favor of the manufacturer, informed the judge, and adjourned. After three days and a final morning of deliberations, the initial seven-vote majority in favor of the manufacturer became a nine-vote majority, and the trial was over.

Auto Trial 2
The second auto trial where we interviewed jurors involved another rollover accident. In this case, the rollover happened when a rear tire on a sport utility vehicle blew out while the vehicle was traveling at highway speeds. After the blowout, the driver lost control of the vehicle and steered off of the road, which caused the vehicle to roll over. During the rollover, the driver lost his life. The plaintiff's estate argued that the vehicle had an unstable design that caused it to tip over after the blowout. The defense responded that the rear tire that blew out was almost bald and should never have been on the vehicle in the first place. Although the trial lasted four weeks, the deliberations took just one day.

After electing a foreperson, each juror stated where he or she stood on the case. Five people favored the plaintiff, while seven supported the manufacturer. However, few jurors had a very good sense of what actually happened during the accident and how the plaintiff was hurt. As one juror told us, "We didn't really understand how the accident took place. There was never a clear picture presented. Honestly, we didn't get into the whole tipping-over issue." Another juror said, "The tire was so off that I never focused much on the other issues." A third juror stated, "Everyone believed something was wrong with that vehicle. But seven jurors believed it didn't matter in this case because the tire problem wiped out everything else. The seven of us convinced the others that the tire problem blew out the other issues."

As a result of the seven defense jurors arguing that the tire, not the vehicle, caused the rollover, four of the five proplaintiff jurors switched sides when the jury returned from lunch. This gave the defense jurors an eleven-to-one majority, but this trial required a unanimous verdict. Within a few minutes after the four other proplaintiff jurors deserted her, the last juror came over to the defense side and made the vote unanimous. When we asked this juror why she changed her mind so quickly, she said that she agreed with the other jurors "because the tire was the cause of the rollover." "The plaintiff was at fault," she said, "for using that tire." As we probed further, though, this last juror became a little more open about her real reasons for switching sides. "We had sat there all day," she said. "The discussion was getting heated. People were making ad hominem arguments against each other [calling each other names]. I decided that if we didn't reach a verdict that day, the judge would call us back on Monday. Maybe several days would pass before the judge declared a mistrial. I didn't want to go through that, so I switched sides." In other words, the verdict in this trial was reached because seven jurors couldn't understand much of the evidence and fixed on a simple story that a bad tire caused the accident. Four jurors found reasons to change their minds after lunch. And the last juror just got fed up and switched sides because she didn't want to have to come back to the courthouse another day.

Auto Trial 3
The third trial where we interviewed jurors was much like the first two. A sport utility vehicle veered off the road when the driver got distracted and had to make a sharp turn to get back on the highway. The vehicle rolled over at a high speed, the roof partially crushed in, and the driver received a severe head injury. The driver sued the automaker, claiming the roof was defective, while the manufacturer blamed the driver's distraction for causing the accident.

As in the other auto cases, immediately after electing a foreperson, the jury turned to the first question on the verdict form, which asked if a defect in the vehicle's roof structure caused the injury. Four jurors said the roof was defective, while eight said it wasn't. The eight jurors thought the driver was injured when his head went out the window during the violent rollover, not when the roof crushed partially into the vehicle. The jury debated this question all morning on the first day of deliberations. After lunch, one proplaintiff juror switched sides: "The defense jurors convinced me that the defendant's version of how the injury happened was more accurate than the plaintiff's version." "Also," she added, "I didn't want to return on Monday." Thus, the original eight-to-four majority quickly became a nine-to-three majority, which was enough to declare a verdict. But before the jury foreman could inform the judge that a verdict had been reached, another proplaintiff juror suddenly said he had changed his mind, as well, and now favored the defense. According to several jurors we interviewed, this man had been a "strong advocate of the plaintiff's position." One juror said," Everyone was surprised when he switched." Another juror said the man who switched at the last minute "just wanted to be on the winning side." As if this sudden switch were not enough, another plaintiff-leaning juror revealed during his interview, "I would have changed my vote, too, if we had needed another vote."

These three auto trials reveal several ways that groupthink and storytelling affect actual deliberations. First, the original majority vote became the final verdict in each case, demonstrating the informational influence of the majority's story about what caused the accident. Second, in each case, enough jurors in the minority eventually switched sides, so the jury would have a sufficiently large majority to reach a verdict and go home, reflecting the normative influence of groupthink. And third, when the facts were unclear, a simple story was able to trump complicated evidence and satisfy enough jurors to declare a verdict.

At this point, you may have concluded that groupthink inevitably turns jurors into a flock of sheep, with confused jurors acquiescing to the majority. In the final chapter of this book, I discuss several ways to overcome groupthink, so that minority views, or stories, are heard more clearly.

Confusion about Language and Terminology

In addition to informational and normative forces affecting jurors' verdicts during deliberations, jurors' verdicts are also shaped by an often-tortured process of deciphering the legal language of the judge's instructions and the verdict forms. "What exactly are we supposed to be doing now?" jurors often ask each other. Few jurors are familiar with legal terminology. Many are not college educated, and some are not high-school graduates. For others, English is second language. Yet they must all parse the finer points of legalese.

For example, when we interviewed jurors about their deliberations after another rollover trial, we learned that the jurors were unable to answer a key question on the verdict form because they couldn't understand what it was asking them to decide. The question asked if any negligence by the vehicle's driver was the "proximate cause" of the driver's injury. *Proximate cause* basically means the "most likely cause of an event." In other words, "Did the driver's negligence cause his or her injury?" Yet the verdict form defined *proximate cause* in the following way: "In order to be a proximate cause, the act or omission complained of must be such that an ordinary person or corporation using ordinary care would have foreseen that the event, or some similar event, might reasonably result therefrom." So opaque was this sentence that the jury debated its meaning for several hours. Finally, the jury sent a note to the judge, asking him to clarify the definition. The judge sent a note back, instructing the jurors to "do the best they could with the definition provided by the court." Doing their best, ten jurors finally decided that the proximate cause of the accident was driver error and that the rollover itself and the resulting injury were just a freak occurrence. This led the jury to decide against the plaintiff and in favor of the manufacturer by a ten-to-two majority.

In a case involving a motorcycle accident, jurors struggled with a similar definitional problem. A question on the verdict form asked the jurors, "Did the [plaintiff's motorcycle] perform as safely as an ordinary consumer would have expected?" Four jurors were unable to decide if "ordinary consumer" pertained to ordinary consumers of motorcycles, that is, motorcycle drivers, or to ordinary consumers who have never driven a motorcycle. One juror said they debated this question "for many hours." Finally, the jury sent a note to the judge asking her to define *ordinary consumer*. The judge replied that the question meant "ordinary consumers of motorcycles." The judge's clarification allowed two of the four uncertain jurors to change their minds and join the majority on this question.

Another linguistic barrier then arose. A further question in the verdict form asked, "Did the [motorcycle] have potential risks that were known at the time of its manufacture, distribution or sale?" Several jurors couldn't understand who was supposed to have known about the risks: motorcycle drivers or average people? After some debate, the jurors unanimously agreed that the plaintiff was an experienced motorcycle rider, and therefore she should have known about the risks of riding a motorcycle. So, the jury decided ten to two in favor of the manufacturer of the motorcycle.

In another case, the jury elected a foreperson and then began deliberations by reading the judge's instructions. A juror told us, "The instructions seemed so contradictory that we spent a long time reading and rereading them but still couldn't understand them. We sent the judge a note, and he told us to read all of the instructions carefully again." Rereading the instructions seemed to clarify some issues, and one of the proplaintiff jurors switched sides, followed by two other proplaintiff jurors. Rereading the instructions made for a nine-to-three majority in favor of the manufacturer, and the jury declared a verdict in favor of the defense.

CHAPTER NINE

Storytellers in Robes

"Jesus, this is the scariest thing I've ever seen." "I never want to go through this again." "Why do I even try cases in front of these kinds of people?" Slumped in their chairs, mouths gaping, heads in their hands, attorneys are often shocked when they watch mock jurors deliberate. Viewed through one-way mirrors or on closed-circuit TVs, typical mock-jury deliberations are far removed from the triers-of-fact ideal embodied in the United States Constitution. As shown in the previous chapter, that seeming nugget of irrefutable evidence; the prestigious expert whose testimony was so hard to schedule; the carefully conducted and expensive accident reconstructions, scientific analyses, and economic projections, all might be ignored by jurors in favor of a vaguely relevant example or anecdote from someone's personal experience. "Surely there must be a better way to obtain a verdict," attorneys often say with a sigh.

You may be thinking the same thing. "Are jurors really capable of rendering just verdicts?" "Wouldn't judges, with their law-school degrees, their experience on the bench, and their expertise in making decisions, be better at resolving disputes than laypeople who know nothing about the law, that is, jurors?"

Legalists versus Realists

If you are asking yourselves questions like this, then you are already dipping your toes into a long-standing debate about judges in America. On one side, the legalists maintain that judges follow strict guidelines and precedents. They determine the law as it applies to the facts. They are guided by previous verdicts and court findings. They keep their personal views out of their decisions. In other words, they follow a strictly legal path to reaching a verdict.

On the other side of this debate, the realists reply that judges are people. Like anyone else, judges view the world through lenses colored by political ideology, race, gender, religion, and life experiences. They rely on familiar cognitive shortcuts that can blind them to differing perspectives. They are mindful of how their rulings may help or hinder their career paths to a higher court. When making decisions with a panel of two other judges, as happens at appellate courts, they yield to group pressure and conform to majority opinion. In other words, from a realistic analysis, judges behave just like jurors. Which side is right in this debate? Do judges strictly follow the law in making decisions, or are they influenced by a host of ideological and personal factors when they make rulings or reach verdicts?

The realists—those who argue that judges are just people and not all that different from jurors—point out that judges frequently disagree among themselves when they interpret the law. "If the law is so straightforward," the realists ask, "so based on codes and precedents, then why would different judges reach different conclusions when they have the same facts?" In this chapter, I show how often judges disagree, what accounts for their disagreements, and whether judges are better than jurors at rendering just verdicts.

When Judges Disagree

To start my analysis of judges reaching different conclusions about the same set of facts, I can provide several projects run by my jury-research firm, using mock judges instead of mock jurors. Sometimes attorneys try cases before a judge instead of a jury. In these so-called bench trials, a judge, not a jury, is the finder of fact as well as the interpreter of the law. A judge listens to each side's evidence, considers the facts, applies the law, and reaches a verdict. Some litigants prefer a bench trial over a jury trial because a bench trial is usually faster than a jury trial. A judge is likely to be better educated than a typical juror. A judge leaves a public record of the decisions he or she has made over a career, which help to predict a judge's ruling. And a judge may seem less likely than a juror to be an unpredictable wild card.

When my firm runs a mock bench trial, we recruit a panel of ten to twelve mock judges. The mock judges are typically retired judges who served in federal or state courts around the United States. These women and men have spent their careers hearing lawsuits and presiding over cases. In their qualifications and experience, they are similar to the real judge whose decision will determine the client's case.

Just as in a mock jury trial, the mock judges hear detailed evidence from each side. Often the judges also receive dense packets of legal briefings and motions beforehand. During presentations from the attorneys, the mock judges are lined up from left to right at a long table on an elevated stage, appropriate for their status and similar to the perspective from which they would hear cases in court. Just as in court, the judges are allowed to interrupt the attorneys, ask questions, and make comments.

After the legal presentations, the mock judges fill out lengthy question-naires, just as mock jurors do. In the questionnaires, the judges answer numerous questions about the case, state their verdicts, and explain why they reached the verdicts they reached. Then the judges deliberate together for several hours in small groups, sometimes respectfully, sometimes less so. After deliberating and listening to each other's reasoning, the judges provide a final verdict on the case. This format allows us to compare verdicts among different judges at different stages in the mock trial and to understand the reasoning behind their verdicts. It opens a rare and unusual window onto the judicial mind, a window that is not available outside this mock judge format.

SatCom v. Rocketron

One of our mock judge trials involved a dispute between a company that made communication satellites and a company that provided rocket launches in order to lift the satellites into orbit around the earth. The satellite com-pany—let's call it SatCom—sued the rocket company—let's call it Rocket-ron—because the satellite company believed the rocket company went back on its word and failed to provide an agreed number of launch opportunities at an agreed-upon price. Basically, SatCom said that Rocketron promised SatCom four launches for its customers' satellites. Then Rocketron broke its promise by selling SatCom's launches to other customers for a higher price. Rocketron replied that SatCom had no satellites ready for the promised launches. What SatCom really wanted, Rocketron argued, was to prevent Rocketron from selling the launches to SatCom's competitors by claiming that the launches belonged to SatCom. In other words, the lawsuit involved a straightforward contract dispute. The question for the judges to decide was, Which party violated its obligations under the launch agreement?

We hired twelve retired judges to take part in this exercise. Actual attor-neys from one of the companies involved in the dispute summarized each side's case before the judges. The exercise lasted for an entire day. The judges filled out a questionnaire telling us their verdicts at several points during the mock trial: first, after the opening statements, when each side gave an overview of its case; second, after the cases in chief, when the attorneys had presented the evidence in favor of each side's interpretation of the contract; and third, after the twelve judges had deliberated in two six-person groups.

At the end of the day, after they had spent several hours conferring together, the twelve judges split six to six. In other words, in what should have been a straightforward interpretation of contract language, half of the twelve judges favored SatCom, while half favored Rocketron. Several judges also changed their minds over the course of the day. After the opening statements, only three judges supported SatCom; after the evidence was presented, five favored SatCom; and after deliberating together, six came to support SatCom. Perhaps more interesting, although we deliberately mixed up the two deliberation groups so that both groups contained some judges who were pro-SatCom and some who were pro-Rocketron based on their questionnaire responses at the end of the day, one of the groups decided unanimously in favor of SatCom, while the other decided unanimously in favor of Rocketron.

When we analyzed the judges' responses to the written questionnaire, we found that those judges who supported SatCom viewed the contract quite differently from those judges who favored Rocketron. One of the pro-SatCom judges said, "Much of the contract's language is unclear and open to interpretations." Another pro-SatCom judge said, "The intent of the contract and a commonsense interpretation favors [SatCom]." A third pro-SatCom judge declared, "[Rocketron] failed to honor the contract." A fourth added his own rationale for what he concluded was Rocketron's failure to honor the contract: "[Rocketron] was in cahoots with [SatCom's] competitors."

A judge who favored Rocketron agreed with the SatCom judges about the vague terms of the contract but came to the opposite conclusion: "I accepted [Rocketron's] interpretation of this poorly drafted contract." Another pro-Rocketron judge concluded, "The history of the negotiations favors [Rocketron]." A third justified his siding with Rocketron by supposing that "[SatCom] was attempting to tie up [Rocketron's] launch schedule in order to deny launches to [SatCom's] competitors." A fourth stated boldly, "There were no weaknesses in [Rocketron's] defense."

In this example of a mock judge trial, a panel of twelve judges split down the middle in their verdicts. Judges on each side came up with their own idiosyncratic theories or made-up stories, such as one party was in cahoots with the other's competitors, to explain the parties' behavior. The judges reached such a conclusion even though no evidence was presented at trial to explain the parties' motivations. And we have seen that, despite what the judges believed about who should win or lose the dispute when they began deliberating in six-judge groups, each group ended up in unanimous agreement—in opposite directions—on each panel. This is strong evidence to support the realists' contention that judges are people, too, just like jurors.

LittleGuys v. ClickSearch

Another mock judge trial that we ran involved small mom-and-pop companies that paid for priority listings on a major web-search engine. Let's call this case LittleGuys v. ClickSearch. The small companies claimed that they were misled by ClickSearch's billing policies, so they were charged more than they expected to be charged each time a web searcher clicked on their listing. The amount of overcharge was tiny for each individual mom-and-pop company, but for the whole category of small mom-and-pop companies, the alleged overcharges amounted to hundreds of millions of dollars. Thus, several mom-and-pops banded together and filed a lawsuit, asking a judge to certify them as representatives of the entire class of small advertisers, each of whom might have been misled by ClickSearch's billing policies. In other words, the mom-and-pops that brought the lawsuit asked a judge to certify their lawsuit as a class-action lawsuit. If the judge agreed to certify the mom-and-pops as representatives of an entire class, then the lawsuit could move forward. The class of small advertisers could then sue the web-search company for hundreds of millions of dollars.

In order to determine how the actual judge who would hear the case would likely rule on this motion for class certification, we recruited a panel of ten retired judges to listen to LittleGuys' claim and ClickSearch's response. The judges had served in state courts and federal courts. Each judge received a thick packet of legal briefings from each side, along with a detailed questionnaire. We asked the judges to read the material carefully, fill out the questionnaire, and tell us their decision on whether LittleGuys should be certified as a class.

Once again, even though the judges read the same material and even though they all were experienced interpreters of the law, the judges disagreed among themselves. Four of the ten voted to certify the entire class of mom-and-pop advertisers. The other six refused to certify the entire class; however, three judges identified a smaller subclass for certification, while the remaining three judges each found a different type of subclass to certify. In other words, among the ten judges, five different classes of small advertisers were identified as capable of suing ClickSearch.

The judges also gave different reasons for their decisions. One judge voted for the entire class because he said a reasonable consumer would have been deceived by ClickSearch's billing policy. Another judge rejected this conclusion and stated emphatically, "Consumers were not misled." When the judges were asked to decide whether testimony by a marketing expert would be helpful to clarify how a reasonable consumer might interpret ClickSearch's billing policies, the judges split down the middle. Five judges would have admitted testimony from the marketing expert, and five would not have admitted such testimony. In reaching their decisions, one judge clearly reasoned from his own personal experience, "People knew when they got their bill what was going on." In other words, if the mom-and-pops simply read their monthly ClickSearch bills more closely, then they would not have been deceived.

I could show other mock judge studies that my consulting firm has run over the years, but there would be similar results. Judges disagree among themselves. Or they agree but for different reasons. Or they rely on a story from their personal experience to justify their decisions, such as "People should have read their bills more closely." Examples like this make it hard to deny the claims by legal realists that judges are people and, in fact, think very much like jurors. But there are more than anecdotal examples to support the view that judges are people. In the following chapter, I provide several empirical studies of judges' biases in interpreting the law and the facts in different types of disputes.

How Judges Shape Trials and Influence Verdicts

These two examples involved bench trials, when a judge was both the finder of fact and the interpreter of the law. But even in jury trials, when jurors are mandated by the Constitution to be the finders of fact, judges wield great power over the facts that jurors see and hear and, hence, over the outcome of the trial. From this perspective, every trial is in some way a bench trial. And every trial is in some way subject to the vagaries that different judges bring to the task of judging.[1] The following are some ways that judges' decisions shape the course and outcome of a jury trial.

Discovery
Discovery is the process through which attorneys discover the evidence to be presented at a trial. Typically, they do so by interviewing witnesses who were present at a murder scene in a criminal trial, for example, or by obtaining the opinions of various experts on automobile design in an auto accident case or

by combing through thousands of pages of research reports, medical tests, and internal e-mails in a drug-safety case.

Judges influence the discovery process by deciding how much time attorneys can spend on discovery, how many witnesses and experts they can interview, how long the interviews can be, which topics can be covered in an interview, and which documents a company must turn over for inspection. Each of these decisions determines which facts jurors will hear. And control over the facts amounts to control over the verdict.

Pretrial Motions

A motion is when an attorney submits a written request to the judge, asking the judge to rule on key issues in a trial. A motion to dismiss asks the judge to dismiss the trial altogether because there is insufficient credible evidence for a jury to hear. If a case is dismissed, then it never goes before a jury.

A motion for summary judgment asks the judge to rule on which aspects of a case can be presented to a jury and which must be excluded. A summary judgment ruling often narrows the scope of a trial dramatically. It may rule out a request for punitive damages, for example, because in the judge's mind there is no evidence of malice or willful indifference by the manufacturer of a product. By ruling on which aspects of a case can be presented to a jury, the judge can significantly strengthen or weaken one side's case over the other.

A colorful example of such a ruling comes from a trial in Cook County, Illinois. The trial was about whether an auto accident happened because of a design defect that was allegedly foreseeable by the engineers who designed the vehicle. If the plaintiff could establish that a foreseeable defect caused the accident that injured the plaintiff, then the jury would have to consider awarding substantial punitive damages to the plaintiff.

The attorney representing the vehicle manufacturer filed a motion with the judge, requesting a ruling that Michigan law should apply to this case, even though the trial was taking place in Illinois. The reason Michigan law should apply, the attorney argued, was because all the engineering work that allegedly resulted in the defective design occurred in Michigan. Precedents clearly supported such a ruling, he noted. If the judge ruled in favor of allowing Michigan law to apply, however, then the ruling would have benefited the automaker because Michigan law did not allow a jury to award punitive damages in such a trial.

After the attorney argued his motion in favor of Michigan law, the presiding judge complimented the attorney on his argument. The judge then ruled against the attorney whom he complimented and gave his reason for overruling the attorney as follows: "The good people of Cook County did not elect me to apply Michigan law to an Illinois accident, counsel."

A similar incident happened in southern Texas, near the Rio Grande Valley. An automaker was sued because it had not installed as standard equipment in all its vehicles a certain safety feature that was technically feasible at the time. Most people knew each other in the small town where the trial was being held. Many were unemployed. And the local court had a reputation of being quite favorable to plaintiffs in lawsuits. A scholarly out-of-state attorney appeared before the local judge to argue in behalf of a motion filed by the automaker. The motion basically argued that federal law prevented the lawsuit from going forward in the state court because a federal court had already decided that the manufacturer was not required to have installed the safety feature in question merely because it was feasible to do so.

The out-of-state attorney had been warned by local lawyers that the judge did not have much sympathy for out-of-state automakers and their attorneys. Despite the warning, the scholarly out-of-state defense attorney approached the bench, greeted his honor, and introduced himself. "What are we here for?" the judge gruffly asked. The attorney began to explain the motion he would be arguing, and the judge cut him off. "Oh yeah, I remember," the judge said. "This is the one where you're trying to tell me that the poor, injured, and maimed people I'm here to protect shouldn't have their day in court. Do you have anything to add?" The defense attorney made his argument in support of the automaker's motion. The plaintiff's attorney said a few words in opposition to the defendant's motion, and the judge quickly denied the defendant's motion on the spot.

After a judge has decided which aspects of a case can be presented to a jury, the judge then determines how the case will be presented. On the night before a trial is set to begin, or even on the morning at the start of a trial, attorneys on both sides invariably submit additional motions to the judge, asking the judge to exclude certain evidence because it may be prejudicial or to restrict a particular witness's testimony or part of the testimony because it may be hearsay or misinformed or beyond the witness' expertise. Through such rulings, the judge once again acts as a gatekeeper over which facts a jury will hear.

An example of such a last-minute ruling comes from a trial in Lowndes County, Alabama, a rural area south of Mobile that is notoriously biased against out-of-state defendants. On the morning the trial was set to begin, the defense filed 23 motions, totaling some 150 pages, arguing that the plaintiffs should not be permitted to present certain evidence and testimony to the jury because it was prejudicial. Ordinarily, the plaintiffs would respond to each of the twenty-three motions, submitting detailed arguments against each motion and stating a rationale for why the plaintiffs believe the evidence and testimony in question should indeed be presented to the jury. Ordinarily, the judge would then review the twenty-three motions and responses and rule on each one. The published trial schedule provided ten days for such motions to be considered by the judge. But on that morning in Lowndes County, Alabama, the pace of justice was not ordinary. Within a few hours of the filing, before the plaintiffs had filed a single response to the defendant's twenty-three motions, the defense attorney received a fax from the court. The fax simply stated, "Defendant's motions filed today are denied."

Jury Selection

After a judge rules on the various motions that determine which facts a jury will hear and how the facts will be presented, the judge then rules on who will hear the facts. During the process of jury selection, the judge rules on whether jurors must fill out a written questionnaire and which questions can be included in the questionnaire about the jurors' backgrounds, beliefs, and values. The judge rules on whether the attorneys may conduct oral voir dire or whether the judge will conduct the voir dire on behalf of the attorneys. If the judge allows the attorneys to conduct the voir dire, then the judge rules on how much time the attorneys can spend questioning individual jurors about their potential biases related to the case. If an attorney wants to strike a juror because the juror already appears to favor one side or the other before even hearing the evidence, then the attorney asks the judge to strike the juror for cause. The judge either grants the attorney's request or refuses.

In my experience as a jury consultant, these cause challenges often seem to reveal a judge's own biases. For example, in a typical auto-accident case, a juror might admit during voir dire that he or she had owned a similar vehicle in the past and had experienced a similar problem with the vehicle. "I'm just not sure I could be fair," a juror might confess to the attorney who is conducting the voir dire, "because of my past experience with this vehicle." "Your honor," the automaker's attorney would say to the judge, "I move to strike juror 7 for cause." The judge then turns toward the juror and gravely asks, "Do you mean, madam, that you would not follow my instructions to keep an open mind and refrain from reaching a conclusion until you have heard all of the evidence?" Chastened, the juror replies, "Oh no, sir, I will do my best to keep an open mind." "And you will not allow your past experience to influence your decision in this case," the judge further intones. "No sir, I'm sure I can be impartial." "Juror 7 is not excused," the judge announces, thereby leaving a juror on the panel who appears to be clearly biased against one of the litigants.

An attorney friend has told me that such cause challenges are especially fertile grounds for bias to reign because judges have huge discretion in these matters: "Judges know their rulings will almost never be overturned because it is so hard for appellate courts to conclude that a trial judge has abused his or her discretion." The attorney added, "I can think of many instances—in fact, it is harder to think of a trial where it did not happen—where judges ruled one way or another on a cause challenge, and it was clear to all that the ruling was based more on which side the judge thought the juror would favor or whether the judge liked or disliked the potential juror."

A more extreme and more unusual example of judicial interference with the makeup of the jury comes from a civil trial in Miami. According to one trial attorney who was there, "Halfway into a month-long trial, the judge called a female juror up to the bench. The juror was a successful, well-off, well-educated owner of an architecture firm, someone whom both sides expected to favor the defense. With no warning to any of the attorneys, and without seeking arguments from either side, the judge told the woman she was being excused because he had seen her sleeping and he didn't think she was paying enough attention to the evidence to be able to deliberate fairly." Even the plaintiff's lawyer, who may well have benefitted by a possibly defense-leaning juror being removed from the jury, told the defendant's attorneys that he was "stunned" and "baffled" by the judge's move. According to the attorney who related this story to me, "None of the attorneys recalled having ever seen the woman sleeping. The judge just made that up." In the attorneys' minds, the judge's removal of the architect was a blatant attempt to influence the outcome of the trial by changing the makeup of the jury.

Trial Presentation

Once the trial begins, the judge exerts further control over the facts a jury will hear by the rulings he or she provides on attorneys' objections to witnesses' testimony or attorneys' arguments. "Sustained" or "Overruled," the judge intones when an attorney jumps up to challenge the line of questioning by an opposing attorney or the statements made by a witness.

Judges' rulings on graphic presentations are becoming extremely important in the electronic age. In an auto-accident case, for example, both sides often try to present a jury with a highly sophisticated graphic reenactment of how they believe the accident occurred. Looking almost like a video game, the staged electronic reenactments can appear so real that they virtually replace the disputed incident in a juror's mind. A judge must rule if these reenactments fairly represent the circumstances of the real accident. Likewise, crash-test videos of a vehicle's tendency to rollover may be so vivid that they unfairly strengthen one side's case over the other, even if they seem obviously staged. A judge must rule on whether such crash-test videos can be presented to the jury without improperly biasing the jury.

Jury Instructions and Verdict Form

The last thing jurors hear before they retire to deliberate are instructions about the law that the jurors must apply. Although the impact of these instructions is debatable because they come so late in the game and are often so abstruse as to be nearly indecipherable, they can have a major impact on jurors' deliberations under the right circumstances. Recall the instructions given to jurors in the Trayvon Martin murder trial, when the judge reiterated the essential elements of Florida's Stand Your Ground law: "The danger facing George Zimmerman need not have been actual; however, to justify the use of deadly force, the appearance of danger must have been so real that a reasonably cautious and prudent person under the same circumstances would have believed that the danger could be avoided only through the use of that force." These instructions may have simplified the jurors' task and tilted uncertain jurors toward favoring the defendant, Mr. Zimmerman.

After deliberations, jurors fill out a verdict form about their decision and return the form to the judge. But as shown earlier, jurors often begin their deliberations by reading the verdict form aloud and polling one another to see if they agree on how to answer the questions in the form. Consequently, the wording and order of the questions in a verdict form can have a significant influence on jurors' deliberations. Attorneys typically vie over the phrasing and order of the questions in a verdict form, and the judge must adjudicate their differences.

Chapter Summary

Retired judges in mock trials can differ significantly among themselves about how to interpret contracts and whether to certify a class of plaintiffs as having common interests in suing a defendant. In support of these different interpretations, different judges see the facts of a case differently. And different judges even make up different stories to support their interpretation of the facts. This amounts to strong support for the realists' view of judges' decisions over the legalists' view. In other words, judges function much like other people, such as jurors.

Unlike other people, however, judges' rulings have far-reaching implications for which facts a jury will hear, who will comprise a jury, what is permissible evidence for attorneys to present during a trial, and how the instructions and verdict forms will be worded.

In the next chapter, I examine which factors lead judges to see the same facts differently. Can a judge's race, gender, and political philosophy affect that judge's views of the law? When judges reason together, are they influenced by fellow judge's comments and majority pressures—similar to the informational and normative influences that affect jurors' deliberations? Do judges take mental shortcuts, just like jurors, that can blind them to alternative interpretations of the law and evidence? Should we necessarily trust a judge or some other professional "decider" to reach better decisions than jurors?

CHAPTER TEN

The Biases behind Judges' Stories

If judges are truly impartial—as they instruct jurors to be—then why would judges differ among themselves when they see the same evidence in a bench trial? Shouldn't they all reach the same conclusions about the facts? And if judges are truly able to listen to all the evidence with an open mind—as they instruct jurors to do—then why would judges' rulings on motions regarding evidence, experts, or jury selection ever appear to reflect the judges' personal views about who should win a lawsuit? Could it be that judges' decisions are shaped by their demographic characteristics, history, ideology, beliefs, lifestyles, and cognitive limitations, just as jurors' verdicts are? Is this why judges may reasonably be viewed as storytellers in robes? In this section, I examine several recent studies that have connected judges' rulings with their backgrounds and beliefs. I show how judges take the same type of mental shortcuts that jurors take when they make decisions about the evidence.

The best studies of judicial bias have focused on federal judges. It's easy to connect these judges' beliefs and backgrounds with their judicial decisions. Unlike state court judges, who are generally elected by voters in the judges' venues, federal judges are appointed by the president of the United States. If both senators from the appointee's state do not approve the appointee, then they can block or hold up the appointment. Then the entire US Senate has to approve the appointments. This means that a long paper trail accompanies the appointments of federal judges. We know the political party of the president who appoints the judges; we know the political party of the two senators, who, by senatorial custom, must be consulted in the appointment; and we know the political parties of the senators who vote to approve or disapprove the appointment, when Senate approval is required, as for Supreme Court justices. Because presidents do not generally appoint judges whose views are different from their own, and because senators do not generally approve judges with whose views they disagree, we can assume that the political parties of appointed judges are similar to the political parties of the appointing president and the approving senators. In addition, we have newspaper editorials about the appointees' backgrounds. And we often have the appointees' own voting records on lower courts where he or she served.

When we know the political party of an appointee's supporters and we read newspaper editorials about an appointee's background and values, and we have an appointee's prior voting record on lower courts, we can easily infer an appointee's ideology. It is not hard, then, to relate a federal judge's ideology and background to the judge's decisions on cases that come before him or her. When the cases involve ideologically tinged matters, such as civil rights, affirmative action, individuals or unions suing businesses, or the government challenging corporations, a judge's ideology and background become especially telling.

Supreme Court Justices

The US Supreme Court is the top tier of federal judges. Once they decide a case, their decisions are irreversible, except by the Supreme Court itself, and they become the law of the land. The appointment of Supreme Court justices requires approval by the US Senate, and here is where the importance of a justice's ideology first appears. We know from the acrimonious debates surrounding approval of Supreme Court justices the importance of a justice's views on such controversial matters as abortion. Senators very seldom vote to approve a Supreme Court justice who does not reflect their own political ideology.

Statistics make the case crystal clear. The authors of the book *The Behavior of Federal Judges* compare the decisions of Supreme Court justices appointed by Republicans with those appointed by Democrats.[1] First, the authors look at the judges' decisions when they served on lower courts, before they were elevated to the Supreme Court. This comparison shows that justices appointed by Republican presidents were significantly more conservative in their prior decisions than justices appointed by Democratic presidents. Then the authors compare the verdicts of Supreme Court justices by political party. Data going back to 1946 show that Supreme Court justices dissent among themselves on about two-thirds of the cases that come before them; they agree only about one-third of the time. When the justices dissent, they generally dissent on ideologically tinged cases, such as those involving civil liberties, women, minorities, and individuals suing the government and businesses. On civil liberties cases, for example, conservative justices are three times more likely to vote conservatively than are liberal justices. So pervasive are the ideological differences between justices appointed by Democrats or Republicans that the authors conclude that Supreme Court justices "often make up their minds before oral argument, that is, before the lawyers have completed presenting their case. Indeed, their minds will often be made up when they decide, long before oral argument, to hear the case."[2] Supreme Court justices, then, seem to function just like jurors, telling a story early in a case, perhaps before the case was ever argued, and then arriving at a verdict consistent with their stories.

Appellate Court Judges

The US Courts of Appeals are the second-highest courts in the country, just below the Supreme Court. Because the 179 judges in the 13 courts of appeals can hear many more cases that the 9 judges in the Supreme Court, decisions by appellate court judges often become the final law of the land, unquestioned and unreversed by any other court. For this reason, appellate court judges, who serve a lifetime appointment, are extremely powerful and influential.

In 2016, seventy-six judges on the courts of appeals had been appointed by Republican presidents and ninety-four by Democratic presidents, with nine vacancies. Most of the time, appellate court judges hear cases in three-judge panels, with the judges on each panel randomly assigned from all of the judges in the circuit. Important decisions by appellate court judges are almost always published. This makes it quite easy to connect a judge's ideology (as defined by the political party of the president who appointed the judge) with how often a judge votes conservatively or liberally on cases that he or she hears. If a judge's ideology had no influence on his or her decisions, then there should be no difference between the number of liberal and conservative decisions of Republican-appointed judges and Democrat-appointed judges.

The fact that judges sit in three-judge panels also makes it easy to assess how the ideology of the other judges on a three-judge panel influence each judge's decision. For example, a panel may randomly contain one Republican-appointed judge and two Democrat-appointed judges or two Republican-appointed judges and one Democrat-appointed judge or three Republican-appointed judges or three Democrat-appointed judges. If the ideology of the other judges on each three-judge panel has no effect on an individual judge's decisions, then there should be no difference in how often a judge votes conservatively or liberally in differently composed panels.

Two recent studies, however, reveal that an appellate court judge's ideology can, in fact, exert a strong influence on his or her decisions.[3] In cases where a judge's ideology is likely to come into play—for example, cases dealing with abortion, affirmative action, campaign finance, capital punishment, race, sex, disability discrimination, and environmental regulations—there is a clear difference in the decisions of judges appointed by Republican presidents versus those appointed by Democratic presidents. On the average, Republican-appointed judges reach conservative decisions 61 percent of the time. Democrat-appointed judges reach conservative decisions 47 percent of the time. In other words, Republican-appointed judges are about one-third more likely to reach conservative decisions than judges appointed by Democratic presidents.

The influence of an appellate court judge's ideology becomes much stronger when other judges on the three-judge panel share the same ideology. When a Republican-appointed judge sits with two other Republican-appointed judges, the odds of a judge reaching a conservative decision rise to 66 percent. In contrast, when a Democrat-appointed judge sits with two other Democrat-appointed judges, the odds of a judge reaching a conservative decision fall to just 37 percent. As astonishing as it is, these figures mean that the random assignment of judges onto three-judge appellate court panels can influence the outcome of the panel's decisions by almost 50 percent!

These studies reveal not only the effect of a judge's ideology on a verdict but also the susceptibility of appellate court judges to the influence of peers—that is, the beliefs of the other judges on the three-judge panel. Judges are much more likely to vote their ideology when their fellow judges on the three-judge panel hold the same worldview. "Does this mean," you might ask, "that judges on the second-highest court in the land behave much like jurors when they deliberate together? Are appellate court judges subject to the same informational and normative influences that affect jury deliberations?" Apparently so.

According to the authors of one of the studies on appellate court judges' decisions, at least two psychological phenomena may be going on. First, as the judges in the three-judge panels talk, their like-minded positions reinforce each other, and each judge's position becomes more similar and more extreme or more polarized. And second, as the judges listen to their colleagues' opinions, they tend to shift toward the majority position—that is, they conform. In other words, appellate court judges behave very much like jurors: Their votes reflect their ideologies and worldviews, and they are influenced by groupthink.[4]

District Court Judges

District courts are the third tier of the federal judiciary. There are 89 district courts for the 50 states and 678 district court judges in 2016. District courts are the workhorses of the federal court system. District court judges preside at bench trials, administer jury trials, rule on which evidence can be presented in court, and sentence criminals within limits set by Congress. Although district court judges are appointed by the president and serve for life, the decisions of district court judges can be reversed by appellate court judges. District court judges also do not serve in panels of three, as do appellate court judges. Therefore, ideology appears to play a less significant role in the decision of district court judges—with a few glaring exceptions. In a recent study of more than a half-million criminal defendants, Republican-appointed district court judges sentenced black defendants to three months longer prison time than Democratic-appointed district court judges.[5] In organized-drug-crimes cases, district court judges appointed by Republican presidents sentenced defendants to six and a half more months in prison than Democrat-appointed judges. In cases involving individual drug dealers, Republican-appointed judges sentenced defendants to almost four and a half more months in prison than Democrat-appointed judges. And in weapons cases, Republican-appointed judges sentenced defendants to three and a half more months in prison than Democrat-appointed judges.[6]

In 1988, when nearly two hundred federal district court judges had to give their opinions on new sentencing guidelines in criminal cases, a key difference arose between the judges who were more or less likely to endorse stiffer mandatory criminal sentences. District court judges with backgrounds as criminal defense lawyers were more likely to oppose the stiffer mandatory penalties. According to the authors of this study, judges with backgrounds as criminal defense attorneys may have had a shared worldview that made changes in sentencing guidelines "uniquely provocative" to them.[7] The authors also found that African American district court judges were more likely than white judges to oppose mandatory sentencing guidelines as a violation of an individual's right to an individually imposed criminal sentence rather than a sentence mandated by external guidelines. In other words, African American judges seemed to take more of an individual-rights approach to sentencing criminal defendants than did non–African American judges. While the influence of a judge's ideology or worldview seems to have less impact on decisions in district courts than in appellate courts or the Supreme Court, there is still evidence of ideological voting. According to the authors of *The Behavior of Federal Judges*, "ideology influences judicial decisions at all levels of the federal judiciary."[8]

Federal Judges' Cognitive Illusions

Federal judges' decisions not only reflect their political ideologies, biases, lifestyle, and ethnicity, but they also incorporate the same types of cognitive illusions that influence juror's verdicts. As explained in chapter 4, the human brain evolved to jump to conclusions based on limited data, to interpret new situations based on familiar situations, and to take a variety of mental shortcuts in order to decide a course of action. We might think judges would be immune to such cognitive illusions and biases because, after all, they are experts in judging. But recent research on judges' decisions suggests that judges behave much like jurors when confronted with new information. According to the authors of the article "Inside the Judicial Mind," "[w]holly apart from political orientation and self-interest, the very nature of human thought can mislead judges confronted by particular types of situations into making consistent and predictable mistakes."[9]

In November 1999, almost two hundred federal magistrate judges attended a conference in New Orleans. Magistrate judges are something like assistant federal district judges. They are selected by district judges based on qualifications and merit to perform many of the functions that district judges perform. Magistrate judges handle criminal proceedings, preside over pretrial conferences, conduct civil trials, and enter final judgments in cases where the litigants agree to accept the magistrate's decision. At the New Orleans conference, the judges were asked to read brief descriptions of several lawsuits and give their opinions about who should win the lawsuit and how much in damages to award. Here are the facts from one of the lawsuits the magistrate judges read:

> Suppose that you are presiding over a personal injury lawsuit that is in federal court. The defendant is a major company in the package-delivery business. The plaintiff was badly injured after being struck by one of the defendant's trucks when its brakes failed at a traffic light. Subsequent investigations revealed that the braking system on the truck was faulty and that the truck had not been properly maintained by the defendant. The plaintiff was hospitalized for several months and has been in a wheelchair ever since, unable to use his legs. He had been earning a good living as a freelance electrician and had built up a steady base of loyal customers. The plaintiff has requested damages for lost wages, hospitalization, and pain and suffering but has not specified an amount. Both parties have waived their rights to a jury trial.[10]

Half the judges were simply asked, "How much would you award the plaintiff in compensatory damages?" The other half were told that the defendant had moved to dismiss the case because the damages would not meet the minimum of $75,000 required by law for the case to come before the court. The judges were asked to rule on whether the motion should be denied and, if not, to award the amount of punitive damages that they believed was justified by the injuries and losses.

The important point to note here is that $75,000 is obviously far too small an amount of damages to compensate the plaintiff for his accident, permanent injuries, loss of income, and inability to perform his job as an electrician for the rest of his life. The figure of $75,000 provides no real information and, in fact, can be seen as an insulting denial of the plaintiff's true injuries and losses. Yet, strangely, the judges who heard the $75,000 figure awarded about $350,000 less in damages than the judges who heard no figure at all. What's going on here? Why would professional judges who heard an absurdly low figure that conveyed no information award 30 percent less damages to the plaintiff than judges who heard no figure at all?

The explanation for this strange phenomenon has to do with something psychologists call anchors. Anchors affect judgment by changing the standard of reference that people use when making numeric judgments: "Even when people conclude that an anchor is not accurate, mentally testing the validity of the anchor causes people to adjust their estimates upward or downward toward that anchor."[11] A more bizarre example comes from a study of judges in Germany. Here, judges with more than fifteen years of experience on the bench were asked to read a summary of evidence from a criminal trial involving a shoplifter. Then the judges threw loaded dice that always came up with a total of three or nine, depending on the dice. Next the judges were told to award a sentence they believed was appropriate to the shoplifting crime that they reviewed. The judges who threw dice that totaled three sentenced the defendant to five months in prison on average, but the judges who threw dice that totaled nine sentenced the defendant to eight months in prison. That's a difference of three months in prison, all determined by a random throw of loaded dice![12]

A very similar phenomenon happens with jurors. Numerous studies, as well as our own mock-trial experience, show that jurors tend to rely on anchors when they award damages to plaintiffs. In one study, for example, when a plaintiff's lawyer requested $100,000 in damages to compensate his client for injuries and losses, the jury awarded $90,000. Yet, in the very same case, when the plaintiff's lawyer requested $500,000 in damages, the jury awarded nearly $300,000. Anchors create cognitive illusions by creating a context for making judgments, even when the information in an anchor is useless or irrelevant.[13] And anchors affect both jurors and judges.

Another cognitive illusion that affects both jurors and judges is hindsight bias.[14] Once someone hears that something has happened in the past, they overestimate the likelihood that it was bound to have happened again. They unrealistically believe that the event was foreseeable, both by themselves and by others. In one study, a group of mock jurors heard about a case where a midwestern city was sued by a group of residents for not having been better prepared to prevent serious flood damage from a nearby overflowing river. Two groups of mock jurors heard exactly the same facts about historic flood records, possible precautions to prevent damage, and how tax dollars spent on flood control could prevent flood damage. One group then heard about an actual flood that caused serious damage to residential property in the city.

Which group do you think was more likely to find the city liable for not having taken adequate precautions to prevent flood damage? Remember, both groups heard exactly the same information about what the city knew when it decided how much money to allocate to flood control, but only one group heard about an actual flood. Despite having heard exactly the same information, the mock jurors who also heard about the flood were much more likely to find the city liable for not having taken adequate precautions to prevent flood damage. From the perspective of hindsight, this group overestimated both the likelihood of a flood and the city's ability to foresee and prepare for a flood.

Judges are no different. At the New Orleans conference mentioned previously, nearly two hundred magistrate judges were asked to read the details of a lawsuit filed by a prisoner against the director of the state prison where he was incarcerated. The prisoner said he was seriously injured by negligent medical treatment at the prison. When the case was dismissed by the district court, the prisoner asked the court of appeals to rule on his complaint. One-third of the judges was told that the court of appeals dismissed the case; another third heard that the court of appeals sent the case back to the lower court for reconsideration; the final third was told that the court of appeals overruled the lower court. At this point, regardless of which ruling the magistrate judges had heard about, they were asked which of the three possible rulings they personally believed the appeals court should have made from the three legally permissible options.

How do you think these experienced judges saw the case? Did each judge rely on his or her understanding of the facts of the prisoner's case and the law pertaining to those facts? Or did the judges follow whatever they were told the court of appeals had ruled? It turned out that most of the judges agreed with whatever they were told the court of appeals had ruled: most of the judges who heard that the appellate court dismissed the case decided to dismiss the case; most who heard that the appellate court decided to send the case back to the lower court decided to send it back; and most who heard that the appellate court overruled the lower court's ruling decided to overrule.[15] Were the magistrate judges' rulings influenced by hindsight bias? Or conformity pressures? Or simple expedience?

Anchoring and hindsight bias are just two examples of typical cognitive illusions that affect both judges and juries. Other examples of cognitive illusions that affect judges have been documented, as well. According to the authors of "Inside the Judicial Mind," a systematic review of the evidence on judicial decision making leads to the conclusion that judges are human:

> Even highly qualified judges inevitably rely on cognitive decision-making processes that can produce systematic errors in judgment. . . .
>
> Unlike the rest of us, however, judges' judgments can compromise the quality of justice that the courts deliver.[16]

Are judges aware that their decisions may be biased by nonlegal factors? A study by a Harvard Law School professor and his colleague goes a long way toward answering this question.[17] They asked 32 US federal judges to read a set of legal briefs and case facts about a foreign military general who was convicted by the International Criminal Court for the former Yugoslavia of committing war crimes during the Serbo–Croatian War in the 1990s. The general was appealing his conviction, and the judges were asked to decide whether to uphold or overturn his conviction.

Half the judges read about a similar case decided by the same court that provided a strong precedent for upholding the general's conviction; the other half read a decision by the same court that suggested a weaker precedent for overturning the general's conviction. Because judges rely heavily on precedents when making a ruling, it was reasonable from a legal perspective to predict that the US federal judges who read about the strong precedent to uphold the conviction would have upheld the general's conviction. Likewise, it was reasonable from a legal perspective to predict that the judges who read about the weaker precedent to overturn the general's conviction would have leaned toward overturning the conviction. However, what makes this study interesting is that the same judges who heard about the respective precedents also heard a bit of legally irrelevant information. Half the judges heard that the general who was accused of war crimes had no regrets about the horrors of the war; the other half heard that the general felt deep regret about all of the bloodshed.

How do you think the judges ruled? Did they follow the precedents provided by similar cases and decided by the same court to either uphold or overturn the general's conviction, depending on which precedent they read? Or were they influenced by the legally irrelevant information about the defendant's lack of remorse about the war crimes (in one version) or by his deep regrets (in the other version)? When nearly one hundred law professors at America's top law schools were asked this question, they overwhelmingly predicted that the precedents would have a much stronger influence on the judges' rulings than the legally irrelevant information about the two defendants. But if you have followed the arguments of this book, you will not be surprised that the law professors were wrong. The precedents had almost no effect on the judges' rulings. On the other hand, 87 percent of the judges who read about the remorseless defendant voted to uphold his conviction, while only 41 percent of the judges who read about the regretful defendant decided to uphold his conviction! The legally irrelevant information had a much stronger impact on federal judges' rulings than the precedent cases that the law professors expected to matter.

But this isn't the end of the story. When the US federal judges were asked to explain the reasoning behind their rulings, they focused mainly on the precedents and almost entirely disregarded the legally irrelevant information. The judges seemed to be unaware of the factors that had most influenced their decisions.

How Do Judges Compare with Jurors as Decision Makers?

One of the oldest questions in the psychological research about jury behavior is whether judges and jurors view trial evidence similarly and reach similar verdicts. Originally, this question was approached by asking trial judges to review all the cases they had tried for several years and to indicate whether they agreed with the respective jury verdicts. Most of the time, the judges said they agreed with the jurors. But this type of long-after-the-fact agreement could have been marred by judges' faulty recollection of the evidence, as well as hindsight bias—or even by a desire to make the jury system look good.[18]

A better approach is to ask judges to state their own "verdicts" while the trial jury is deliberating. This way, the judges' "verdicts" cannot be tainted by their knowledge of the juries' verdicts. Several studies of both criminal and civil trials used this approach and found that judges arrived at the same verdicts as jurors more than three-quarters of the time.[19] The clearer the evidence was, in the judges' views, the more likely were judges and jurors to agree. As reassuring as this finding is, it is unclear when in the trials the judges came to the same verdict as the jurors did, to what extent judges relied on stories in appraising the evidence, and whether the type of people on the jury panel affected the degree of judge–jury agreement.

For example, do judges arrive at a story that drives their verdicts early in a trial, just as jurors do? Or do judges wait until they have heard all evidence and then decide? If the evidence matters more to judges than to jurors, then we might expect judges to wait until they have heard all evidence before making up their minds. But if judges and jurors make up their minds at different points in a trial, then wouldn't we see more disagreement between judges and jurors? Could it be that judges, like jurors, actually make up their minds early in a trial and return to this "verdict" at the end of a trial? From this perspective, the high rate of judge–jury agreement might reflect the fact that both judges and jurors operate under the same types of biases. Thus, they reach the same verdicts at the same points in the trial.

Regardless of how often judges agree with jurors on trial verdicts, judges and jurors still do *not* agree on almost one-quarter of the cases in which they hear the same evidence. Some researchers think jurors are more lenient with certain criminal defendants and certain types of civil defendants than are judges.[20] It is tempting to ask, "Who is more fair when judges and jurors disagree?" But as I have shown repeatedly, the facts of a lawsuit are a matter of who is appraising the facts. Apparently judges and jurors see the facts differently about one-quarter of the time.

Chapter Summary

Judges disagree among themselves because judges, like jurors, can be biased by their political ideologies, their ethnicity-related attitudes and experiences, and cognitive shortcuts. Conservative judges rule differently from liberal judges; white judges rule differently from African American judges; judges with backgrounds as prosecuting attorneys rule differently from judges without such a background. Judges' sentences can be affected by random cognitive anchors, legally irrelevant information, and hindsight bias. And just like jurors, judges are susceptible to groupthink when they talk to like-minded colleagues, when informational and normative pressures to conform lead them to more extreme decisions. Moreover, judges' frequent agreement with jurors' verdicts seems to suggest that both judges and jurors may be influenced by similar information.

Having established that professional judges are not necessarily fairer and less biased than jurors and thus may not qualify as a desirable replacement for juries, let's look in the next chapter at the near-extinction of trial by jury in America. Why has the number of jury trials plummeted to historical lows? What are the consequences of allowing jury trials to vanish? Can—and should—we prevent the demise of trial by jury?

CHAPTER ELEVEN

The Vanishing Jury

Imagine some friendly visitors to America—from Europe or Asia or even from Mars—who are seeking to comprehend the American legal system. Upon arrival they turn on the TV news in their hotel room and scan the newspaper slipped under the door and find both saturated with accounts of square-jawed wife murderers, egomaniacal corporate executives and freakish entertainers on trial. Unsurprisingly, our visitors readily conclude that the trial is the central pivot of the American legal system. If told that actually the trial is rapidly disappearing from the American legal scene, our [visitors] might be incredulous. Yet there is an abundance of data that shows that trials, federal and state, civil and criminal, are declining precipitously.

So said Marc Galanter, a professor at the University of Wisconsin School of Law, when he spoke at the symposium "A World without Trials."[1] Other commentators have described jury trials as "dwindling," "disappearing," "obsolete," and an "endangered species."[2] Some have gone so far as to pronounce the death of the jury trial in America.[3] Are we really about to witness the death of trial by jury in America? Here is how the number of jury trials—both civil and criminal, in federal courts and state courts—has plummeted over the past few decades. You decide for yourself if the jury trial is about to become a relic of history.

Federal Civil Trials

Today, less than 1 percent of all civil cases filed each year in US federal courts ever reach a jury. This means that, of all the cases where corporations sue each other or an individual sues a corporation or an individual sues another individual, less than 1 percent are tried by a jury of one's peers. To put that figure in perspective, fifty years ago, 12 percent of the cases filed in federal courts went to a jury; hence the phrase the "vanishing jury."[4]

State Civil Trials

It turns out to be much harder to compare the number of civil trials that go before a jury in state courts from one year to another. Different states keep trial records differently. But 98 percent of all jury trials occur in state courts, not federal courts, so state courts provide a much broader measure of the decline in jury trials.

In states where the majority of the US population lives, only about 0.5 percent of all civil cases filed in a year go before a jury today—just as low as in federal courts.[5] In Texas state courts, for example, the number of civil jury trials dropped by two-thirds between the mid-1990s and the early 2000s. A Texas lawyer who generally represents businesses and manufacturers in court described the steep drop in the state's jury trials as an "unhealthy trend for those seeking justice." "Unfortunately," he predicted, "this trend is going to continue."[6] Or, as other commentators have observed, the "civil trial is approaching extinction."[7]

Federal Criminal Trials

The picture is hardly different for criminal trials in federal courts. Today, about 2 percent of all criminal cases filed in federal courts in a year ever reach a jury. Fifty years ago, by comparison, more than 15 percent of criminal cases filed in federal courts in a year were heard by a jury. A federal judge in New York recently resigned from the bench after more than twenty years because she had so few trials to judge. "Trials are way down," she said. "The [courthouse] is quite dead."[8] Criminal jury trials are disappearing almost as fast as civil jury trials.[9]

State Criminal Trials

In state courts today, only about 3 percent of all criminal cases filed in a year go to a jury. Compared to forty years ago, that's a drop of more than 60 percent. While the decline in the portion of criminal trials reaching a jury in state courts is not yet as steep as in federal courts, the trend is moving in the same direction, "close to the vanishing point," according to Marc Galanter.[10]

Long-Term Trends

"Not so fast," you might say. "Even if the proportion of civil and criminal cases that reach a jury today is close to the so-called vanishing point, there were never that many jury trials in the first place. How can a phenomenon that was never really there vanish?" According to Lawrence Friedman, a professor at the Stanford Law School, the jury trial was never the norm in American justice. The percentage of criminal cases that reach a jury has been declining for more than a hundred years, he says. Most criminal felony cases, such as robbery, brawling, check forgery, and petty drug deals, have always been fairly routine and were generally handled through plea bargaining. Less serious misdemeanor cases, such as vagrancy, drunkenness, and prostitution, seldom involved lawyers at all, much less a jury.[11]

The same is true for civil cases. When trains and streetcars began sharing streets with pedestrians, the number of slip-and-fall accidents jumped dramatically. But the companies who operated the trains and streetcars settled cases quickly with cash payments. Other common civil complaints, such as nonpayment of debts, evictions, property disputes, or arguments between neighbors, were handled by judges and seldom came to trial. Historically, Professor Friedman says, "trials were the exception, not the rule."[12]

Even if trial by jury was never the rule in American justice, Marc Galanter points out that the proportion of lawsuits heard by a jury began slowly dropping in the first half of the twentieth century and then accelerated dramatically in the late 1980s. What accounts for the long, slow decline in jury trials and then the sudden plunge?

The Long Decline in Jury Trials

One of the main reasons for the decline of civil jury trials over the past one hundred years was a historic shift from the trial itself to the pretrial preparation period. Recall from chapter 1 that the role assigned to the jury in the United States Constitution was to decide questions of fact. Traditionally, after a complaint, or a pleading, was filed, a jury would be assembled; it would listen to the evidence, deliberate, and reach a verdict. There was no pretrial discovery. Neither side could force the other side to produce potentially incriminating letters or documents for examination. Neither side could question the opposing party or the other side's witnesses in advance to see what they would allege at trial. Judges had no role in investigating the facts and determining their accuracy. As a result, neither side had a very clear idea of what the other side might present during the trial. This potential surprise factor often caused problems. If some completely unexpected piece of evidence was presented, then it was not possible for the surprised side to halt the trial, conduct additional discovery, and reconvene the jury. What the jury saw was what the jury got.[13]

All of this began to change in the 1930s, and the changes were codified in 1938 in the Federal Rules of Civil Procedure, which state courts adopted, as well. Under the new rules, parties in a lawsuit had a right to demand to see the other side's relevant records and documents in advance of a trial. Parties could submit questions to each other that each side had to answer "fully in writing under oath." And each side had the right to confront in person the party filing the lawsuit, question each other's witnesses, and conduct oral depositions that had to be recorded. Although these pretrial procedures were intended to make trials fairer and more efficient, in practice they seem to have had the opposite effect.

According to John Langbein, a professor of law and legal history at Yale, the new emphasis on pretrial procedures ended up not "enabling" the jury trial but "displacing" the jury trial. It shifted the focus from the jury, as finders of fact, to the judge, as case manager, gatekeeper of facts, determiner of admissible evidence, approver of depositions, and encourager of litigants to settle lawsuits instead of bringing them before a jury. As Professor Langbein puts it, "The discovery system has transferred into the pretrial process much of the work of eliciting facts and refining legal issues that had formerly been the function of the trial." The pretrial process became a full-scale dress rehearsal for the trial, minus the jury. But as Professor Langbein laments, "Having seen the dress rehearsal, today's litigants often find that they can dispense with the scheduled performance" (i.e., the trial).[14]

Summary Judgment

One of the tools that emerged from the new Federal Rules of Civil Procedure was something called summary judgment, briefly discussed earlier. After each side's evidence has been obtained and reviewed during pretrial discovery, one or both parties can petition the judge to dismiss the entire case or to dismiss certain claims or to ban some evidence. One of the parties will claim that the other side's evidence or the law supporting the other side's case is not strong enough to justify a jury trial. If the judge agrees, which often happens, then the judge can dismiss the case. Of course, summary-judgment rulings can be appealed, but a judge can reaffirm his or her initial ruling and often does. As a result of summary judgment, the case may never reach a jury. During the last twenty years, resolving a case by summary judgment rose from under 2 percent of all cases filed in federal court to almost 10 percent—a fivefold increase. In some judicial districts, almost one-quarter of all cases filed are resolved by summary judgment.[15]

Settlement

The other and more important tool to emerge from the 1938 Federal Rules of Civil Procedure is known as settlement. In a settlement, both sides agree to end a dispute, generally for an exchange of money. Typically, the plaintiff accepts less money than its lawsuit demanded, and the defendant offers more money than it thinks the plaintiff deserves. The parties agree to settle on an outcome that both sides may believe is less than satisfactory.

Sometimes the parties settle a lawsuit because of the sheer costs and time consumed by conducting discovery, preparing witnesses, and taking depositions. It's easier and less risky to settle a case and move on than it is to spend all the money to prepare for trial and an uncertain verdict. In other cases, settlement results from a judge helping the parties reexamine their claims, reevaluate the strength of their evidence, and reassess their demands for damages. At least one federal judge has admitted in writing, "Federal judges tend to be biased toward settlement."[16]

According to Professor Galanter, judges' bias toward settlement reflects a profound change that occurred in the 1970s. Judges came to see their role, not as moving cases toward trial, but as resolving disputes during the pretrial period, typically through settlement. So committed were judges to settlement that pretrial conferences between the judge and the litigants could become almost coercive. Settlement conferences came to be called "cajolery conferences" or "muscle mediation."[17]

When the judge is unable to bring about a pretrial settlement, the opposing parties often carry out an elaborate dance, full of thrusts and feints and offers and counteroffers, up to the very last minute. Often a blizzard of motions is filed in the final days before a trial, requesting the judge to eliminate one of the claims in a case, to prohibit a certain line of testimony, or to disqualify the other side's expert. Late-night phone calls are made between the competing attorneys, in which the plaintiff may offer to accept a few million dollars less to settle the case or the defense may offer a few million dollars more if the plaintiff will settle. Sometimes, this dance goes on even through jury selection, as the parties wait to see if they will obtain an unusually favorable jury in their view or if the jury looks determined to cut no slack to one side or the other.

I have seen more than a few cases settle after a jury has been selected and the judge is about to begin the trial. "May counsel approach the bench, your honor," one side's attorney will ask the judge. After a few whispered comments at the bench, the attorney extends a hand to opposing counsel, and an agreement is reached to settle the lawsuit. The plaintiff has decided to accept less money or the defendant to offer more. The case is formally resolved before the trial begins, and the jury is never seated.

In criminal trials, the pretrial parallel to settlement is plea bargaining, and it means exactly what it sounds like. A defendant accused of a crime can bargain with the judge by waiving a jury trial and agreeing to plead guilty in exchange for being charged with a less serious offense or receiving a lighter sentence. Plea bargaining is the reason that so few criminal cases ever reach a jury today.

The Recent Steep Decline in Jury Trials

Even though jury trials have been declining for decades, over the last few years, something different has happened. The long descent became a steep drop, as though the road to resolving disputes veered off the edge of a canyon and careened into a chasm where jury trials hardly existed. A major reason for the dive was the emergence of something called alternative dispute resolution (ADR). ADR is basically an alternative justice system in which arbitrators, mediators, and private judges replace federal and state courts and juries. It's like a detour away from jury trials.

Arbitration

Ever read your cell-phone contract? Here are the terms and conditions a Sprint customer must accept, as listed on Sprint's website:

> PLEASE READ THIS CAREFULLY; IT AFFECTS YOUR RIGHTS
>
> Mandatory Arbitration and Waiver of Class Action. Instead of suing in court, you and Sprint agree to arbitrate all Disputes (as defined below) on an individual, non-representative, basis. You agree that, by entering into this Agreement, you and Sprint are waiving the right to a trial by jury or to participate in a class action or representative action. This agreement to arbitrate is intended to be broadly interpreted. [W]e each agree that all issues regarding the Dispute are delegated to the arbitrator to decide . . .
>
> An arbitrator's award will be a written statement of the disposition of each claim and will also provide a concise written statement of the essential findings and conclusions which form the basis of the award. The arbitrator's decision and award is final and binding.

No Trial by Jury and No Class Action

IF FOR ANY REASON A CLAIM ARISING OUT OF OR RELATING TO
THIS AGREEMENT IN ANY WAY PROCEEDS IN COURT RATHER
THAN IN ARBITRATION, REGARDLESS OF WHETHER THE CLAIM IS
AN ACTION, COUNTERCLAIM OR ANY OTHER COURT PROCEED-
ING, WE EACH AGREE THAT TO THE EXTENT ALLOWED BY LAW,
THERE WILL NOT BE A JURY TRIAL OR CLASS ACTION AND WE
EACH UNCONDITIONALLY WAIVE ANY RIGHT TO TRIAL BY JURY.

Is that clear enough? By agreeing to a Sprint contract, you unconditionally
waive your right to trial by jury to resolve any dispute between you and
Sprint. The Sprint contract is not unusual. Rental-car agreements contain
similar language, as do numerous contracts or agreements whose terms you
accept on the web when you check the little box that says "Agree." When
you undergo medical treatment, join a health club, move to a nursing home,
hire a contractor, or order products online, you often waive your right to
a jury trial without even knowing it. Many employment contracts require
that any dispute between the employer and the employee must be resolved
by arbitration. We have no choice but to accept these terms. Waivers of a
person's right to trial by jury go a long way in explaining what has happened
to the jury trial. As a culture, we are waiving the jury trial out of existence.

As the Sprint contract explains, in arbitration, there is no judge or jury.
Instead disputes are decided by a technically neutral third-party arbitrator in
a more informal process than in court. Like a judge, however, the arbitrator
can award damages and relief, including any attorneys' fees authorized by
law. In arbitration, the rules of evidence are relaxed, the arbitrator's decision
is binding, and there is no appeal of the arbitrator's decision. In many cases,
the arbitrator doesn't even have to give a reason for his or her decision.
Although it's hard to know exactly how many civil cases go to arbitration
each year, the American Arbitration Association, which tracks many but
not all legal arbitrations, reports that the figure has risen from under one
thousand, fifty years ago, to about twenty thousand today. Among disputes
that involve $25,000 or more in damages, about 20 percent go into arbitra-
tion instead of jury trials.[18] A federal judge has described the rapid rise in
arbitration as a substitute for trial by jury as a "trend fraught with danger."[19]

Arbitrators are usually former attorneys or judges. Some arbitrations
involve a single arbitrator, while others include a panel of three, made up of
one person nominated by each side and one neutral. Both have drawbacks.
If it's just a single arbitrator, that arbitrator's binding decision reflects just
one person's view of the case. I had lunch with a very successful arbitrator a

while back, and he told me, whenever he takes on a case, he quickly develops a story about what happened. As I have shown in earlier chapters of this book, stories reflect an individual's personal experience and create filters that can influence verdicts. As for panels of three, I have already shown that three-person panels of judges reflect the political and philosophical biases of the judges as well as peer pressure from the group.

A further problem with arbitration is that it's unclear how neutral arbitrators may be. An investigation by the *New York Times* found that many arbitrators have handled at least ten cases for the same corporate client, which could put the plaintiffs who are suing the corporation at a major disadvantage. Arbitrators have an economic interest in finding for a company who may hire them again instead of finding for an individual they will never see again. Among arbitrators interviewed by the *Times*, more than thirty said the pressure to rule for the companies that give them regular business is real.[20]

Mediation

Another type of alternative dispute resolution is known as mediation. Mediation is when a third party acts as a neutral negotiator between the two sides and helps to bring about a settlement. A mediator's decision is usually nonbinding. A case that is mediated may still go to trial if a mutually agreeable outcome cannot be reached. The goal of mediation, however, is to avoid trial.

Private Judges

The third type of alternative dispute resolution is hiring a private judge. Sometimes called the rent-a-judge technique, this option is used less often than mediation and arbitration, but it offers certain advantages to litigants. The hired judge must be agreeable to both parties. He or she usually brings experience and knowledge about a particular type of litigation. The process involves full discovery and detailed presentation of evidence. The judge isn't distracted by other matters on a federal or state court docket. And the process is faster than jumping through the hoops of a real court. The drawbacks of a private judge are the same as in arbitration. Even if the judge is knowledgeable about a particular type of litigation, the judge is still one person, with personal biases that can't be escaped.

Comparing Amateurs and Professionals

Relying on federal and state court judges, arbitrators, mediators, and private judges instead of juries for a verdict amounts to transferring decision making from amateurs to professionals. But no one really knows if and how professional decision makers differ from amateur jurors. Do they tend to agree with jurors, or do they look for different facts, view evidence differently, and arrive at different verdicts?

A client hired my jury research firm to conduct research to answer exactly these questions. The client needed to make a decision whether to take a case before a jury or a panel of arbitrators. The client, a large corporation, believed that it had been systematically overcharged by suppliers of certain parts for a number of years. Our client wanted compensation for the alleged overcharges. Very large damages were at stake, but the evidence for the overcharge was complex and based on a complicated statistical analysis. The client wondered whether jurors or arbitrators would be more likely to sympathize with its case, reach a verdict in its favor, and award large damages, to the tune of hundreds of millions of dollars.

To answer these questions, we recruited nearly forty mock jurors who were representative of actual jurors in the city where the trial would be held. We also recruited nine professional arbitrators. The mock jurors and the arbitrators heard the exact same hour-and-a-half summary versions of each side's case, presented live in a mock courtroom. Then the mock jurors and arbitrators filled out nearly identical questionnaires about their reactions to the information they heard. Afterward, three twelve-person panels of jurors deliberated together, while three three-person panels of arbitrators deliberated together. How do you think it turned out? Did the jurors and arbitrators agree on a verdict and damages? Or did they differ significantly?

The outcome was quite interesting, in light of this discussion of professional versus amateur decision makers. The arbitrators were more likely to favor the corporation than were the jurors. What's more, the arbitrators who favored the corporation awarded larger damages than did the jurors who favored the corporation.

Why did the professionals and amateurs view the case differently? I believe that each type of decision maker had to fill in gaps in the evidence in order to reach a verdict, and because of their different experiences, they filled in the gaps differently. According to the jurors' and arbitrators' questionnaire responses and to participants' comments during deliberations, the arbitrators found the corporation's statistical analysis of alleged losses complicated and not entirely convincing. But they were used to such analyses, and they were familiar with similar overcharge cases in the past, so they generally accepted the corporation's evidence and awarded large damages.

The jurors, in contrast, took a more commonsense approach. They thought the evidence for the overcharge was not sufficiently clear to justify the huge damages the corporation demanded. And if the corporation was so large and sophisticated and dealt with so many suppliers, the jurors reasoned from a "personal pocketbook" perspective, then why hadn't it been able to figure out that it was being overcharged for so many years? Therefore, the jurors awarded a greater share of blame for the overcharge losses to the corporation itself.

Who was right? The professionals or the amateurs? How you answer this question, of course, reflects your own backgrounds and biases. It also reflects how you feel about jury trials in general. In the next chapter, let's look in more detail at the bad reputation juries seem to have earned and what the losses to society would be if jury trials vanished altogether.

Chapter Summary

The number of lawsuits being tried by juries has been dropping for almost one hundred years. Over the past few decades, the proportion of trials going before a jury has dropped so precipitously that less than 1 percent of civil trials and just a little more than 2 percent of criminal trials are heard by a jury every year. Numerous commentators, including judges and attorneys, worry that the jury may be vanishing altogether.

Criminal trials have been largely replaced by plea bargaining, while civil trials are often settled or replaced by mediation, arbitration, and private judges. Do these alternative approaches adequately replace jury decisions? Professional arbitrators may bring different types of biases to a verdict than do amateur jurors.

The next chapter examines why juries have become so disparaged and distrusted. The chapter asks whether the institutions that have replaced trial by jury can play the same role in American democracy that a jury has played.

CHAPTER TWELVE

Trying the Jury Trial

Several years ago, Patrick Higginbotham, a Dallas federal judge appointed by Republican president Ronald Reagan, declared, "The future of our jury system is very much in danger. There are certain elites in this country who don't trust juries."[1]

Jury Trials Are Too Risky

Beneath the shift from jury trials to summary judgments, judge-managed settlements, trial waivers, and the various forms of alternative dispute resolution is the fact that the jury—specifically a jury of one's peers—is not highly valued today in many quarters. Jurors are viewed as arbitrary, unpredictable, sentimental, unable to comprehend complex information, out of control, biased against corporate defendants, and likely to award immense sums of money for capricious reasons. Many corporations think it is just too risky to try a case before a jury. In Marc Galanter's view, "There is a very real fear of trials."[2]

Galanter goes so far as to suggest that much of American society has a "jaundiced" view of juries. From this cynical perspective, "Indiscriminate suing by opportunistic claimants, egged on by greedy lawyers, and enabled by activist judges and biased juries" is "unraveling the social fabric and undermining the economy."[3] Galanter blames this jaundiced view on heavy media coverage of colorful trials with huge damage awards, such as the McDonald's coffee spill case discussed in chapter 1. Others point to a well-funded tort-reform campaign designed to stop the so-called litigation explosion. This campaign—which has been called "probably the biggest cause of the vanishing jury trial"—has led to laws in many states that limit access to courts and put caps on jurors' damage awards.[4]

Jury Trials Are Too Expensive

Coupled with the perceived risk of jury verdicts is the expense of a jury trial. In a typical civil trial, such as an accident caused by an alleged auto defect, tens of millions of dollars may be at stake, and both sides spend many months on discovery. During judge-sanctioned discovery, the defendant is obliged to plough through years of engineering reports, paper and electronic memos, test-drive results, government-required crash tests, and marketing materials. The plaintiff, in turn, must submit detailed expert opinions about the nature of an alleged defect, alternative tests, and damage analyses to support its complaint. The goal is for both sides to find and surrender to each other anything and everything that remotely has to do with what may have caused or failed to prevent an accident. After receiving each other's materials, both sides then burrow through the mountain of surrendered paper and electronic files in search of smoking-gun evidence.

Both sides hire expensive experts to review the evidence and render opinions about a vehicle's alleged design flaws or the driver's alleged carelessness. Other experts study the accident in order to reconstruct how and why it happened. Still others reenact the accident, subjecting real vehicles to laboratory forces or actual test drives, meticulously documented by electronic devices. Everyone from the allegedly defective vehicle's driver and occupants to accident witnesses, company engineers, and executives are deposed, examined, and cross-examined to see how they will testify in court. Medical experts review the plaintiff's history of postaccident surgeries and treatments and prepare extensive life-care plans regarding projected future treatments. Experts in emotional arguments—that is, attorneys—struggle with how to ask jurors to place an economic value on pain and suffering and on the price of never being able to hold a son or daughter again. And yes, jury consultants, such as myself, are hired to see how the whole thing will play out in front of people who resemble the individuals who will become the real jurors if the case doesn't settle. This pretrial phase of discovery, hiring experts, and taking depositions can run into many millions of dollars. And the real trial hasn't even begun. You can see why settlement might be an attractive option for both sides in a dispute. The dollars alone are enough to encourage a plaintiff or defendant to settle, even in a simple car crash.

Lawyers Lack Experience with Juries

Because so few cases go before juries today, fewer and fewer attorneys are gaining experience presenting information to actual jurors.[5] A senior attorney with whom I have worked for many years and who is one of the best litigators I have ever observed recently complained that he was having a hard time obtaining enough jury trials to train young lawyers. "There's just not much opportunity for them to get trial experience," he said.

Making my friend's point, I recently overheard two young attorneys, both men in their early forties, talk about their trial experience. One worked in a small law firm, the type that in the past would have brought many relatively small claims cases before juries. But he had never faced a jury in his career. The other worked in a regional law firm with a reputation for jury trials. Although this man had helped some senior attorneys prepare for a few trials, he himself had never argued a case before a jury. His sole experience was before an arbitrator. And as already explained, arbitrations seldom involve the extensive presentation of evidence that is part of a jury trial.

Professor Galanter worries that the lack of trial experience among younger attorneys is creating a self-perpetuating pattern. The fewer jury trials that go to court and the fewer attorneys with jury trial experience, the fewer attorneys who want to go before a jury and the more who would rather settle out of court.

Jury Service Is Trying

In addition to the perceived risks and actual costs of taking a case before a jury, the reputation of the jury trial is often besmirched by the experience of serving on a jury. An acquaintance who knows I am a jury consultant was selected to serve on a jury to decide a criminal assault claim in Albuquerque, New Mexico. She couldn't wait to tell me her reactions. "It was the worst experience of my life," she said. "Some of the jurors could barely speak English. Others were on drugs. They ignored the evidence. They wouldn't send the man to prison when he was obviously guilty." Because of this experience, she had signed off on juries forever.

This woman's dissatisfaction with her jury duty is not unusual. An article in the 2008 *Yale Law Review* paints the following picture of jury duty:

> By the late twentieth century, the jury trial had fallen on hard times. . . . As for the general public, the experience of participating in a trial had become a chore. Jurors frequently complained about the poor treatment at the hands of court officials, the inconvenience of jury service, fear over their role as jurors, and anxiety following from uncertainty about the trial process. Moreover, many citizens viewed the jury as archaic, emotional, irrational, and unintelligent. This scorn . . . was hardly without precedent. Mark Twain once said that

the efficiency of the jury system was marred only by "the difficulty of finding twelve men every day who don't know anything and can't read."[6]

Maybe this is why the most common question I get from friends whenever someone receives a jury summon is "How can I get out of jury duty?" No one ever says, "How can I make sure I serve on a jury? It's an important responsibility, and I look forward to the experience." I usually tell people how much they will enjoy serving on a jury, how central it is to our democracy, how ennobling and challenging it is. They typically respond, "I know, I know. But I don't have time. I'm too busy. I can't do it."

What Happens If Jury Trials Disappear?

Should we worry that jury trials are reaching a vanishing point? Or should we accept that jury trials are outdated and move toward a European legal system, where all civil cases and most criminal cases are decided by a judge, not a jury? As trials have gotten longer and more complex, isn't it really wiser to shift toward judges and professional arbitrators to make decisions about disputes that are way beyond the capacity of most jurors to understand? Let's look at the pro and con arguments and try to figure out if there is still a future for trial by jury in American justice.

Several law school professors, judges, attorneys, and even a US senator have written searchingly about a future without jury trials. There are overlaps and differences in their concerns. Together they raise issues that must be addressed before we allow juries to slip away altogether, to become historical artifacts, a constitutional right that few citizens ever experience. The following are the most serious issues, as I see them.

Biased Experts

Before turning trial verdicts over to professionals—judges, arbitrators, and the like—the main question to resolve is whether these pros are less biased than lay jurors in their decisions. The quick answer is "No, they are not less biased; they are differently biased." Recall discussion in the earlier chapters of this book about the role of narratives in people's worldviews. It is almost impossible to set aside fast, story-based analyses of events in favor of slow, systematic evaluations of evidence. In one famous study of expert judgment, a psychologist at the University of Pennsylvania, Philip Tetlock, interviewed almost three hundred individuals who specialized in "commenting or offering advice on political and economic trends." He asked these people to predict the likelihood of certain political and economic events happening in the near future. Then he compared their expert predictions to what actually transpired in the world. The experts' predictions were no more accurate than if they had simply declared every outcome to be equally likely. In other words, their expert judgment was the same as guessing. And the more confident the experts, the more likely they were to be wrong.[7]

Recall, too, the earlier discussion of how the decisions of federal appellate judges are influenced by their political philosophies and the opinions of their fellow judges on three-judge panels. And remember the comparison of the decisions of professional arbitrators with lay jurors in the overpricing case. The arbitrators thought the evidence was murky, but they were willing to side with the corporation because the evidence fit their prior experience with similar cases, while jurors were more skeptical of the evidence. My view is not that experts are biased and jurors are not. It is that we are all biased in our own ways. As Daniel Kahneman says in *Thinking, Fast and Slow*,

> What can be done about biases? How can we improve judgments and decisions, both our own and those of institutions that we serve and that serve us? The short answer is that little can be achieved without a considerable investment of effort. Unfortunately, this is least likely to be applied when it is needed most. The voice of reason may be much fainter than the loud and clear voice of an erroneous intuition, and questioning your intuitions is unpleasant when you face the stress of a big decision.[8]

If individual biases can't be easily avoided, then the obvious corrective is to spread individual biases over more people. Theoretically, the extremes can cancel each other out. A group of varied individuals can foster multiple viewpoints. As Kahneman says, "Organizations are better than individuals when it comes to avoiding errors, because they naturally think more slowly and have the power to impose orderly procedures."[9] But we must add a major "in principle" caveat. As mentioned in a previous chapter, organizations are also subject to groupthink and herd mentalities.

At this point, then, I am strongly in favor of juries over expert judges, mediators, and arbitrators as a means of reining in biases, fostering multiple viewpoints, and grounding judgments in community values. But for juries to work truly effectively, many changes must be made in the ways that information is presented to jurors and in helping juries to avoid groupthink. These needed changes are explored in the final chapter. For now, let's consider additional reasons the vanishing jury may be something to resist and reverse.

A Check on the Power of the State

When juries officially came into being in the eleventh century as part of the Magna Carta, their purpose was to buffer the power of the crown. As explored in chapter 2, in medieval Anglo-Saxon villages as in colonial America, citizen juries (narrowly composed of white males of a certain material worth in the community) had the power to hear cases and reject accusations of the state as embodied by the king or the state. That function continues today in criminal and civil juries. A criminal trial jury can acquit a person accused by the state of committing a crime. A civil jury can find a powerful corporation liable for making and selling an unsafe product, for example, and force the corporation to pay an injured party millions of dollars in damages.

In the American political system of checks and balances, the jury is an important check on the power of the state. Writing in the *William and Mary Law Review*, US Senator Sheldon Whitehouse declares, "The civil jury distributes the divided authority of the state and vests citizens with direct and substantial authority with respect to one of the state's functions: adjudicating disputes both among citizens and between citizens and government officials." He goes on, in rather impassioned oratory, "The premise of the American system of government is that the most powerful in our society will seek to gain control over all exercises of government power. The principles of separation of powers and government by the people, including the civil jury, are our established guardians against such encroachment. We allow them to whither at our peril."[10]

Community Values

In his book *The Death of the American Trial*, law professor Robert Burns argues persuasively that juries reflect community values and the social tensions and conflicts behind such values.[11] An example of this process is the Trayvon Martin case from chapter 5. When a state jury acquitted a community-watch volunteer accused of killing a young, unarmed African American man, the jury acted in behalf of community values. Many of the jurors owned guns or were related to gun owners. The jurors believed that they themselves would have feared grievous bodily harm had they been in the volunteer watchman's situation. The jurors interpreted a Florida self-defense law as allowing the volunteer to defend himself with deadly force. While the jury's verdict may have reflected community values in that part of Florida, the verdict seemed incomprehensible in other communities across America. The verdict ignited widespread discussion of the tensions and conflicts—racial, cultural, political, and personal—behind the verdict. In this way, the Florida jury verdict acted as a public forum for addressing major social questions, in the same way that the Black Lives Matter movement has focused attention on acquittals of police officers accused of shooting unarmed African American men and women.

Law professor Nancy Marder observes in the *Chicago-Kent Law Review*, "One of the reasons for having laypersons decide cases is that they are supposed to rely on their common sense, whether in judging the credibility of a witness or the reliability of evidence, and indeed, the judge so instructs them. Common sense cuts across race, class, and gender; no group has a monopoly on it, and professional training is no guarantee of it."[12] Many of the cases discussed in earlier chapters reflect commonsense influences on jury verdicts. In a civil trial involving an allegedly defective automobile design, for example, a jury must decide from a commonsense perspective if the vehicle's design was unreasonably dangerous, whether a hazard was reasonably foreseeable, and whether a driver used ordinary care in operating the vehicle. People differ strongly in their perceptions of what is reasonable, foreseeable, and ordinary. The same thing is true about whether a breach of contract should be excused or whether a drug's health benefits exceed its risks.

The answers to all of these questions are hammered out during deliberations. At the most basic level, these answers—for good or for ill—reflect the verdicts or the appraisals of ordinary people. The more representative juries are in terms of gender, ethnicity, social class, and life experiences, the more the jury's deliberations reflect community values. When we disagree with these appraisals and the community values they reflect, we should ask ourselves, "Whose appraisals would we rather accept? The community's or the government's?" In the next chapter, I look at a number of possible reforms that can make the jury even more representative of the community.

Personal Narratives
A subtler value of the jury trial is its role as "one of our few official forums for storytelling," according to Professor Robert Burns in his book *The Death of the American Trial*. In the European system, a judge or a panel of judges calls witnesses, determines the facts to be presented, reviews the evidence, and reaches a verdict. In contrast, the American trial is a "place where a citizen can effectively tell his own story publicly in a forum of power. . . . Some of this storytelling will be through the citizen's lawyer, but a trial lawyer is simply a person who knows how to tell an individual's story in a public forum where perspectives other than those of the client have authority."[13] And, as shown in earlier chapters, after the plaintiff and defendant tell their stories, then jurors create their own stories.

Paraphrasing Hannah Arendt, Burns argues that actions produce stories, and to explain what happened requires telling a story. Thus, only stories can give meaning to history. Stories matter because they create a context for the facts. As Burns says, stories "soften" the rigidity and sometimes harshness of written law.

The Power of Stories in a Real Trial

One of the best examples of how a story can soften the rule of law comes from a highly readable description of a murder trial in New York City, including a detailed account of the jury's subsequent four-day deliberations. In the winter of 2000, Princeton historian of science Graham Burnett received a jury summons, reported for jury duty, was selected as a juror, sat through the trial, and at the start of deliberations was elected foreperson of the jury (as we would expect, because he was a white, professional male). His book A Trial by Jury recounts the entire process.[14]

The trial involved the gruesome stabbing death by one man of another during a sexual encounter in a West Village apartment in New York. The defendant said he was lured to the apartment by a man posing as a woman. When he realized the trick and refused an encounter, the defendant said the victim forced him to the floor and tried to rape him. The defendant pulled a knife from his pants, which were at his knees, and, in an act of self-defense, he said, stabbed the other man in the chest and then on the back more than twenty times. When his assailant's grasp weakened, the defendant slipped free, got dressed, and fled the apartment. The state asked the jury to return a verdict of either second-degree murder (a nonpremeditated but intentional killing) or manslaughter (an intentional killing during a heat of passion or unintentional killing due to dangerous conduct).

At his trial, the defendant told this story on the witness stand. Despite the state's intense cross-examination, the prosecuting attorney was unable to shake the defendant. The real problem for the state was a lack of any motive for the alleged murder. According to Burnett, historian of science and jury foreperson,

> It is true that the law did not require proof of a motive (in a second-degree murder trial, only intent to kill must be shown, not the motivation for doing so). But a sane individual, asked to find an apparently mild-mannered person—one with no history of violent crime—guilty of a grotesquely cruel murder, strongly wishes for at least a wisp of a rationale. When none can be offered, it is hard to resist entirely, as beyond doubt, a claim of self-defense.[15]

When the jury retired to deliberate, their opinions were mixed. Nearly all jurors thought the evidence didn't fit together fully, and some favored the defendant, while others leaned toward the prosecution. After three days of often-emotional debate, the jury seemed to be hung. Some of the jurors didn't see how the evidence supported either second-degree murder or manslaughter, but they were also reluctant to find the defendant not guilty. This is when Mr. Burnett stepped in:

> In an effort to reestablish harmony, I offered the following story: those among us who were arguing that we could not let ourselves become slaves to the law were not necessarily arguing against the rule of law itself. . . . The struggle we were having reflected one of the very deepest struggles that human beings had faced. . . . To what degree was the law a thing apart from people—an abstract system laid over the messy reality of individuals and their specific situations—and to what degree did the law emerge from the texture and character of people and the details of their cases? . . . My aim was to give a patina to our conflicts, to dignify the opposing positions with historical mantles so that we could make peace, see intelligence in the opposing views, and rise to the occasion of such a worthy disagreement. . . .
>
> In this, the story succeeded. [One of the jurors] raised his hand and rose to speak. . . . "I believe the defendant did something very, very wrong in that room. But I also believe that nobody has asked me to play God. Justice belongs to God. Men only have the law." . . . [A juror] whispered, "He's convinced me. Justice belongs to God."[16]

By reframing the issue as a story about God's justice rather than men's laws, the jury was able to reach a unanimous verdict of not guilty. As Mr. Burnett observes, "this powerful reformulation—that true justice was God's affair—made it possible to imagine, somehow, that the really important question would remain open." Although I personally believe that this reformulation seems very much like passing the buck to a higher power, it allowed the jury to reconcile both the disturbingly vicious murder and the imperfect evidence for conviction.

In the final pages of his book, Burnett dramatically reveals a fact that potentially justifies the jury's decision to go with their conscience over the law. After the trial was over, the defense attorney told the foreperson that a previous complaint had been filed against the murdered man for posing as a woman to lure a young man to his apartment for sex. The complaint failed to move through the courts, though, because the young man dropped the charges and the judge ruled the complaint as "more prejudicial than probative." If the jury had known this fact, what kind of story would they have then told?

A Civic Culture

A final reason to bemoan the demise of the trial jury would the loss of "one of the great achievements of our public culture." A law professor who has written about the decline of the jury declares, "No other institution of government rivals the jury in placing power so directly in the hands of citizens. Hence, no other institution risks as much on democracy or wagers more on the truth of democracy's core claim that the people make their own best governors."[17] It's easy to hear this declaration as one of those good-for-us civic lessons, but its truth can't be overstated. Far more serious than voting for or against an elected official, a jury trial allows individual citizens to interpret facts and apply the law as they see it. If we allow the jury trial to wane, then we diminish democracy.

A noted defender of trial by jury, Nancy Marder, says the jury trial is a democratizing experience because "it brings together people from different walks of life [and] puts them on equal footing when they arrive at the courthouse. All jurors, regardless of their backgrounds or experience, have one vote and must try to persuade other jurors to their point of view."[18] Running hundreds of mock juries and watching people deliberate on TV monitors or through one-way mirrors, I have been repeatedly struck by how this bargaining process plays out over the course of an afternoon. People of different races who may seldom interact in real life sit at a table face to face and seriously consider each other's views. Alliances form and change, with multiracial groupings on both sides. When someone gets impatient or abrasive, another juror inevitably intervenes to calm things down. Bit by bit, the fabric of democracy is woven more tightly.

Of course, the opposite can happen, too. My friend whose reaction to jury duty I described earlier believed that her fellow jurors were not taking the process seriously and were placing sentiment over facts. For her, the fabric of democracy unraveled a bit because of her jury duty, which raises the greater question of who makes up the peers in a multiethnic, multiracial, economically diverse society like America. This is a question to which I return in the final chapter.

In order to make juries more representative, we the people need to change our beliefs about jury duty. Instead of shuddering when we receive a jury summons or ignoring it until threatened with arrest, we might see the summons with some anticipation as a break in our routines, as a chance to learn something we wouldn't otherwise know, and as an opportunity to enlarge democracy. Part of preventing the decline of the jury is participation in the system.

At the same time, it would be much easier to change our views of participating in the jury system if the system itself were more palatable. Instead of bureaucracy, tedium, and dislocation, the system could encourage and reward citizens for participating. I return to this question in the final chapter, also.

Chapter Summary

There are many reasons trial by jury is disappearing in America. Juries are viewed as unpredictable, trials as too long and costly, arguing before a jury as a job to avoid for attorneys with little jury trial experience, and serving on a jury as an ordeal to escape. But juries also play an important role in our civic culture. Today, as in the twelfth century, juries are a check on the power of the state. Juries are an expression of community values, and controversial verdicts can lead to a reevaluation of community values. Jury service inserts individuals into civic culture and helps democratize society. And jury trials are our only official forum for storytelling, which is how human beings make sense of what happens around us. Thus, there are important reasons to reverse the decline of jury trials and restore trial by jury to a more central place in American justice.

In the final chapter, I turn to whether the American jury trial can be saved and, if so, how it can be saved. I look at across-the-board changes at every level of the jury process. Importantly, I consider how evidence can be presented in a way that respects the information-processing capacity of the human brain rather than ignores it. My hope is that the jury trial in America can be saved. But it will not be easy.

CHAPTER THIRTEEN

Junk the Jury or Fix the Flaws?

A friend of mine is an attorney and highly successful mediator. He takes on major cases, such as airplane crashes with multiple deaths. The task of a mediator, he told me, is to bring both sides of a lawsuit together outside of a courtroom and try to persuade them to accept a mutually satisfying resolution of the dispute. Intending to tweak him just a bit, I asked, "Isn't every successful mediation a jury trial that didn't happen?" Then I added, "And is that good or bad for democracy?" He quickly replied, "It's good for democracy because the jury system is broken." Tweaking a bit more, I asked, "Wouldn't it be better to fix the system rather than abandon jury trials altogether?" My mediator friend conceded that, of course, the system should be fixed. But, as a lawyer who had tried a good many trials before juries, he doubted that the system could be meaningfully reformed. He held such a low opinion of juries that he believed justice would be better served by avoiding juries altogether.

In this final chapter, I examine the question of whether the jury system should be junked or reformed. Are jury trials too antiquated; too unworkable; too expensive; too unsuited for complex cases; and too crippled by prejudice, bias, and incompetence? Or can the jury trial be restored to a central place in American democracy?

In the following pages, I consider various ways to improve the jury system. First, I look at the fundamental concept of a jury of one's peers. What does a *peer* mean in a multiethnic, increasingly class stratified, economically unequal society like the United States? Second, I consider how jury-selection procedures can increase the representativeness of juries and lead to verdicts that the community is more likely to understand as fair and just. Third, I review several changes courts can carry out in order to improve the jury experience and make serving on a jury more rewarding. Fourth, I explore the role of judges to show how they could make trials more efficient and jurors' tasks clearer and easier. Fifth, I focus on attorneys and examine how they could improve case presentations in a way that better respects the capacities of the human brain and helps jurors to understand more clearly what the case is about. Finally, I examine juries themselves to see how they could function better during deliberations. Then we will be in a position to confront the future of the jury trial in America.

How Can We Obtain a Jury of One's Peers?

Before we can decide whether the jury is worth reforming, we first need to ask if it is possible in today's America to assemble a jury of one's peers. The word *peer* comes from the Latin word *par*, which means "equal," and that is the dictionary meaning of *peer* today—an equal. But what would a jury of equals look like in contemporary America? And is a jury of one's equals the same thing as an impartial jury?

Without explicitly acknowledging that jurors are biased, over the last fifty years, Congress has passed laws and the US Supreme Court has issued rulings intended to make federal and state juries look like a "fair cross section of the community." As surprising as it may seem, until the late 1960s, most federal courts drew jurors from a pool known as the "key man system." So-called key men were defined as "men of recognized intelligence and probity" in the community.[1] But relying on lists of key men in order to assemble a jury virtually guaranteed that juries represented a fairly narrow set of biases.

In 1968, Congress passed the Jury Selection and Service Act, which mandated that all litigants in federal courts were entitled to juries selected at random from a "fair cross section of the community."[2] In 1975, the Supreme Court extended this right to state courts, as well. In making this ruling, the court essentially defined an impartial jury as a jury drawn from a pool that looked like a microcosm of the community where the trial was to be held. Subsequent rulings, known as Batson rulings, made sure that jurors representing certain cross-sections of the community could not be eliminated from a jury simply because of their race or gender. Some state courts have added sexual orientation to this list, as well. These rulings have made it even more likely that federal and state juries resemble a true cross-section of their communities.[3]

At this point, you may well say, "Wait a minute! Why should a jury composed of a cross-section of the community necessarily be an impartial jury? Wouldn't drawing jurors from a cross-section of the community almost guarantee that the resulting jury will be a mix of competing interests and perspectives based on ethnicity, gender, education, income, and life experiences? After all, haven't we already seen in previous chapters that both jurors and judges can't help but vote their biases?" Here is how the California Supreme Court sought to answer these perplexing questions:

> [It would be] unrealistic to expect jurors to be devoid of opinions, preconceptions, or even deep rooted biases derived from their life experiences. . . . The only practical way to achieve an overall impartiality [in a jury] is to encourage the representation of a variety of such groups on the jury so that the respective biases of their groups, to the extent that they are antagonistic, will tend to cancel each other out.[4]

Having read this assertion by California Supreme Court justices, you might further ask, "How do competing biases cancel each other out? Wouldn't clashing perspectives lead instead to a quarrelsome standstill?" I believe the answers to these questions require a leap of faith—but a leap that is necessary in a democratic society: Competing biases inspire debate and discussion, as jurors from different walks of life educate each other about their differing perspectives and seek common ground. Such a debate enhances the quality of deliberation. Ideally, jurors leave behind their narrow group interests and arrive at a decision that reflects the interests of the community as a whole. Achieving this ideal, though, requires changing the way information is presented to jurors, clarifying judges' instructions, and teaching jurors how better to deliberate—as I show later this chapter.

The US Supreme Court tackled the question of a jury of one's peers this way in a 1975 ruling: "It must be remembered that the jury is designed not only to understand the case, but also to reflect the community's sense of justice in deciding it."[5] According to the courts, the community's sense of justice is best determined by a wide cross-section of the community. In order to obtain a wider cross-section of the community, we can make the following several changes to the way jurors are selected.

Broaden the Base for Obtaining Potential Jurors' Names

If an impartial jury requires representation from a cross-section of the community, then how do we achieve that wider representation? Specifically, how do we expand the pool of citizens who receive a summons to report for jury duty? Jurors are recruited differently in different states and in different federal court districts. Some states and federal districts rely strictly on lists of registered voters, from which they randomly draw jurors' names. But relying on lists of registered voters means that people who don't register to vote don't get called for jury duty. To broaden the list of potential jurors, other states and federal districts rely on lists of registered voters plus lists of drivers' license holders. To broaden the list further, states like New York draw potential jurors not only from lists of registered voters and drivers' license holders but also from anyone who files state income taxes, anyone who receives unemployment insurance, and anyone who receives some form of family assistance. If our goal is to achieve the widest cross-section of community residents on federal and state juries, then we have to begin by drawing jurors' names from the most diverse and representative lists of community members. This would mean drawing names not merely from lists of registered voters but also from lists of driver license holders, taxpayers, and recipients of state assistance.

Encourage More People to Respond to a Jury Summons

Making juries more representative requires more than broadening the lists from which juror's names are obtained. It also involves making sure potential jurors actually receive their jury summons and respond to them. It turns out that poorer people are less likely to receive jury summons in the mail than people who are better off. Poorer people move more often, have more address changes, and are less likely to report address changes to the post office, so they are less likely to receive jury summons. They are also more likely to ignore jury summons because their employers won't or can't pay their salaries while they serve on jury duty.

On the other end, rich people are likely to ignore jury summons, as well. They might believe they are too busy or jury duty is a disruption in their lives or they don't want to have to undergo the inconvenience of jury duty. A well-off friend of mine once told me that he never responded to a jury summons because he didn't want to take the time out of his life to report for jury duty. Then he received notification in the mail that he would be subject to arrest if he didn't report for jury duty. That changed his tone.

Many states, such as California, make it easy to report for jury duty by allowing people who receive jury summons to call in each morning for a limited number of days and find out if they are needed that day. When the period of eligibility expires, you no longer have to call in, and your jury duty is completed. I, myself, have gone through this process several times. After regularly calling in for several mornings to hear an automated announcement, I was informed that I was not needed for jury duty. Online registration and daily computer updates are another way of notifying potential jurors whether or not to appear for jury duty.[6]

Other states opt not for convenience but for fear. Failure to show up for a jury summons may be treated as an offense. A judge can issue a bench warrant that gives the police the right to arrest you. During a minor traffic stop, the bench warrant can show up on a police officer's computer, and the police officer may well fine you or haul you off to jail. In 2003, in Massachusetts, 48,000 people were fined at least $2,000 each for missing jury duty; in 1999, in Georgia, a music executive spent three days in jail for ignoring a summons; in Arizona, a sheriff's deputy can knock at your door and arrest you for ignoring a jury summons.

Grant Fewer Excuses from Jury Duty

If people show up for jury duty, the next hurdle to assembling a jury of one's peers is the number of excuses requested by potential jurors and often granted by judges. Having been present at scores of jury selections in courtrooms all around the country, I have heard dozens of excuses requested and granted:

"I can't afford to take time off from work."

"My employer won't compensate me for days spent on jury duty [which often pays a token fifteen dollars a day or so]."

"I already have a prepaid vacation that won't be refunded."

"I am the sole caretaker of a child [or an elderly parent or an invalid family member]."

"I can't sit for long periods of time because of a bad back."

"I have to go to the bathroom too often."

"I have poor hearing."

"I don't understand English very well."

"I am a student and would miss too much coursework."

"I am a doctor [or a manager or a supervisor or a teacher] and am essential at my work."

"My religion won't let me judge other people."

"My cousin works in the same office building as one of the lawyers on this case."

Judges differ widely in how they respond to such excuses. Some are quite strict and deny most excuses, telling potential jurors simply to make other arrangements, promising frequent bathroom breaks, or requesting a doctor's note. More than once, I have seen a judge unmask a beseecher who claims not to understand English by asking the juror a rapid-fire follow-up question in English. When the individual responds to the judge's question, revealing an adequate comprehension of the English language, the judge smiles, the jury room chuckles, and the requested excuse is denied. Other judges, especially those elected by the public and facing an upcoming reelection, seem routinely to accept almost any excuse. After all, they want to get reelected.

When judges are too lenient in excusing people from jury duty, the resulting jury pool may look quite unlike the community at large. For example, there will be too many unemployed people, homemakers, or retirees; too many workers at government agencies, which are required to provide employees time off for jury duty and pay normal salaries while employees serve their jury duty; and too many lower-level workers, whose time at work is less essential.

In order to make juries more representative of the community at large, two changes should be made in seeking and granting excuses. First, people should seek fewer excuses. Instead of reacting with a groan and a shudder when a jury summons appears in the mail, one could say, "Wow! I might get to be on a jury! How cool is that?" Of course, to get this reaction, reporting for jury duty must be made more pleasant: fewer needless hours should be spent waiting in drab hallways for a judge to begin jury selection; jurors should be more fairly compensated; trials should be expedited (in ways I consider later); and a juror's task should be made easier through the types of reforms I suggest in subsequent sections. The second change that should be made is granting fewer excuses. I believe judges should be stricter, granting excuses only in the most extreme circumstances. The judge's goal should be to encourage people to participate in the jury system, not to allow them to escape this most basic of civic responsibilities.[7]

How Can We Speed up the Jury Trial?

Critics of the trial jury often complain that trials are just too long, which makes them too expensive, too tedious, too unwieldy, and too inconvenient for jurors. In this section, I look at several proposed changes to shorten and expedite jury trials.

Encourage Judges to Nudge Disputes toward Shorter Jury Trials

Many analysts of the jury system have noted that both federal and state judges tend to manage cases toward settlement instead of toward a jury trial. Settlement allows litigants to avoid the costs and uncertainties of a jury trial. It also frees judges from weeks of sitting in a courtroom. But instead of trying to resolve cases through settlement, judges can also use their power to make jury trials shorter, simpler, and clearer.[8]

For example, in advance of the trial, judges can meet with both sides' attorneys to narrow the issues that will be tried before the jury, set deadlines for submission of evidence, limit the number of experts called by each side, determine the topics about which experts will testify, and issue deadlines for submission of expert testimony.[9] During the trial, judges can limit the time attorneys spend on voir dire, jury selection, opening statements, and closing arguments.[10]

Require Jurors to Fill Out Written Questionnaires before They Appear for Jury Selection

A previous chapter discusses the role of written questionnaires during jury selection. Asking jurors to fill out written questionnaires before they undergo voir dire greatly speeds up the jury-selection process. Jurors can fill out the questionnaires the day before jury selection begins. The questions can probe a jurors' feelings, experiences, and opinions about important issues in the case. The attorneys will have an afternoon or evening to analyze the questionnaires. When the trial begins, both side's attorneys, as well as the judge, will know from a jurors' own words how the juror feels about case-specific issues. Rather than wasting time asking jurors general questions about the litigants, the attorneys will be prepared to bore down on a juror's attitudes and experiences that are pertinent to the case. With detailed written questionnaires, jury selection can be made much more rational and efficient.

Allow Fewer Peremptory Strikes to Remove Potential Jurors from a Jury

Remember that attorneys can remove, or strike, potential jurors from serving on a jury for two reasons. The first reason is for cause. A juror may be struck for cause if the juror seems too biased to provide an objective verdict. For example, if a case involves an auto company, it's not unusual for a juror to say something like, "I used to own one of that company's cars, and it was a total lemon. I'll never buy one again." When this happens, the attorney will no doubt ask the judge to strike that juror for cause because the juror is likely to be biased against the auto company. I believe such an avowed bias is generally a valid reason for removing a potential juror. It is the second reason for striking a juror that can be often be misused.

The second reason to remove a potential juror from a jury is a peremptory strike. The dictionary defines *peremptory* as "brusquely imperious."[11] When an attorney removes a juror with a peremptory strike, the attorney is basically saying, "I'm doing this just because I want to." Using the auto example again, an attorney for a plaintiff suing an auto company might want to strike an older, well-educated, white man who is a car buff because the attorney might worry that the man would be too sympathetic toward the auto industry.

Or the attorney might want to remove an individual with a strong personality because the person might be expected to wield too much influence over other jurors. Or an attorney might remove someone simply because he or she believes, "That type of person has never liked me." However, as discussed earlier, jurors may not be dismissed through a peremptory strike merely because of the jurors' race, gender, or (in some states) sexual orientation.

The number of peremptory, or "just because," strikes is limited by the judge. Some judges allow only a small number of peremptory strikes, while other judges allow six to nine. There is a good argument that the number of peremptory strikes should be limited to just a few or perhaps eliminated altogether. Peremptory strikes basically create a less representative jury than would be achieved without such strikes. For this reason, many commentators have urged the elimination of all peremptory strikes.[12]

How Can We Make It Easier for Jurors to Reach a Just Verdict?

The core of a jury trial is the presentation of evidence to jurors in such a way that they can fulfill their role as triers of fact and reach a just verdict. This requires two key tasks from both the attorneys and the trial judge. First, the attorneys must present each side's facts clearly enough for the jurors to understand the issues and determine responsibility. And second, the judge must explain the applicable law simply enough for the jurors to decide the nature of the alleged violation and the penalties or damages that can be reasonably awarded.

In my experience, both attorneys and judges often do a poor job at these tasks. Over the years, I have observed a surprising number of attorneys give obtuse and rambling opening statements in mock trials; I have heard and read countless impenetrable judges' instructions to juries; and I have reviewed the findings of numerous research projects assessing the quality of opening statements and judicial instructions. This leads me to conclude that the bizarre and unpredictable verdicts we read about in newspapers are seldom the fault of so-called runaway juries; rather, they are more often the fault of unclear presentations of the facts by attorneys and confusing instructions from the judge. Therefore, in this section, I go into some detail about how attorney presentations and judge's instructions can be improved.

Simplify the Judge's Instructions and Move Them to the Beginning of a Trial

Remember from earlier sections of this book that the jurors' role is to appraise the facts of a case, while the judge's role is to instruct the jurors on the law.

In an auto-defect case, for example, the judge will instruct jurors on the legal meaning of such terms as *defect, ordinary care, proximate cause, negligence,* and *gross negligence.* It is the jurors' job to decide if the automaker manufactured and marketed a vehicle with some sort of defect; if the automaker failed to use ordinary care in making and marketing the vehicle; if an alleged defect was a proximate (or direct) cause of an accident and injury; if the automaker was negligent in making and marketing the vehicle; and if the automaker deliberately ignored evidence of a defect and thus was grossly negligent.

Usually, the judge delivers his or her instructions on the law at the end of the presentation of evidence, before jurors retire to deliberate. The instructions are typically stated in lengthy, multiphrase, complicated sentences, full of words that make sense to an attorney but that an ordinary person would view as legalese. The judge reads the instructions, which can easily take from fifteen minutes to a half-hour. Often the judge supplies a written copy of the instructions for the jury to take with them into the jury room. If the judge does not supply the jury with a copy of the instructions at the outset, the jury may request a copy during their deliberations.

Despite the gravity of the judge's legal instructions, my experience observing mock trials and conducting post-trial jury interviews suggests that jurors frequently ignore the judge's instructions. If the instructions are mentioned at all during deliberations, they are often misunderstood, or they are interpreted so as to support what the jurors have already decided, before they heard the instructions.

Many law school professors and psychologists suggest that the judge's instructions could be much clearer and more effective if they were simplified and moved from the end of the trial to the beginning. In one study, for example, people were asked to read either the official Missouri instructions about the law governing capital punishment verdicts or a simplified set of instructions with a flow chart. Then the people were tested about their understanding of the two versions. Those who heard the simplified instructions had a much clearer understanding of the law governing capital punishment verdicts than those who read the official state version. The same thing happened when the issue involved complex damage awards.[13]

Why are standard judge's instructions, delivered at the end of a trial, so difficult for jurors to understand and use as a guide in their verdicts? One of the most thoughtful writers on the trial jury, Jeffrey Abramson, had this to say about typical judge's instructions:

Modern jury procedures mask a charade: we have judges go through the motions of instructing jurors on the law and tell them they must abide by the instructions, but we suspect that jurors do not fathom the instructions and fall back on their own gut reactions or common sense in deciding how the case should come out. To anyone who has ever witnessed a judge instructing a jury, it is clear that our system does not even pretend the instructions are meaningful. Rarely are jurors even provided with written copies of instructions; little attempt is made to translate jargon into common language.[14]

To get around these problems, Dennis Devine, a psychologist who has studied juries, has two proposals: First, "whenever possible," he says, "judges should provide instructions to jurors prior to hearing the evidence. Consistent with the principles of human learning, pre-instruction creates a cognitive framework that helps jurors to prioritize and process the evidence during the trial."[15] In other words, jurors would know what evidence to look for during the trial and how to evaluate it if they heard the instructions before the evidence was presented rather than after the presentation was all over. Devine's second proposal relates to the clarity of the judge's instructions:

> It is abundantly clear that jurors struggle with understanding their instructions, despite what they tell outsiders or even themselves. Lawmakers in some jurisdictions are beginning to act on this reality and rewrite instructions to eliminate the worst aspects of legalese, but this is not a widespread occurrence as yet. Wherever possible instructions should be simplified—not dumbed down but revised to be more comprehensible. The key mechanism for bringing this about is using words and sentence structures that make sense to jurors as opposed to attorneys.[16]

Present the Evidence in a Narrative Format

As mentioned earlier, jurors tend to construct a story when they hear the evidence in a case. Typically, the story involves stored scripts about events in a juror's life that are similar to the issues in the trial. This rush to tell a story occurs because the human brain evolved to engage in fast, narrative-based System 1 thinking instead of slow, analytical System 2 thinking. And it is very difficult to prevent jurors from constructing a story about what really happened in a case before they have heard all the evidence. In fact, up to 80 percent of jurors reach a verdict or begin leaning toward one side after the opening statements. This tendency of jurors to construct a story about the evidence early in a trial has led several observers of jury trials to suggest that evidence should be presented in a more narrative format.[17] Devine asserts that the opening statement should really be thought of as the opening story. He goes on,

It is difficult to think of a trial where it would not be advantageous to provide an overview of one's case before the jurors start hearing the evidence. Providing a general overview is probably more important than fleshing out the specifics. In general, anything that makes it easier for jurors to compose a narrative framework should be done. Under most circumstances, this would include summarizing points in chronological fashion and identifying the motives of major characters in the story.

Likewise, Devine explains, the evidence should be structured in a way that "fosters a cohesive narrative explanation." And the closing arguments "should include a recap of the story."[18]

Two of the most active psychological jury researchers, Neil Vidmar and Valerie Hans, make the same point: "Long before they embark on their deliberations, jurors are attempting to organize the evidence into a narrative account and to test the coherence and consistency of each side's story."[19] Another researcher echoes this point: "Jurors who fail to construct a coherent story that relates to the emerging evidence risk confusion and misdirection. . . . This suggests that more needs to be done to provide jurors with a coherent factual framework in the early stages of the trial and with a clear outline of the legal structure into which the facts must be fitted."[20] The more philosophical Robert Burns declares, "To say what is always requires telling a story; narrative reflects or supplies the necessary order of things."[21]

Teach Attorneys How to Present Narrative Opening Statements

If we take seriously the theory and research on the importance of a narrative opening statement, then it is absolutely essential to make the opening statement into a story. We have no choice. Yet it is extremely rare for attorneys to present opening statements in a narrative format. Law schools seldom teach the importance of storytelling; instead they teach the value of evidence. Consequently, attorneys have traditionally viewed the opening statement as an opportunity to present an overview of the evidence that will follow during the examination and cross-examination of witnesses. As noted earlier, the overview often devolves into a checklist, ticking off a series of names, details of evidence, numerous PowerPoint diagrams, and arbitrary conclusions.

In contrast to this approach, when my jury research firm assists attorneys in preparing for trial, we draft straightforward, narrative opening statements. We organize the opening statements around five points that tell the story of the case, with a beginning, middle, and end. We use five points because one of the most frequently cited studies in psychology, "The Magic Number Seven Plus or Minus Two," shows that the human brain can track just a handful of items at any one time in "tabletop" memory.[22] The more complicated the items, the fewer that can be juggled at once. Hence, our legal stories contain five clear points.

After a brief introduction to the case, we lay out the five points in succession, "just as if you were telling your aunt about the case over Thanksgiving dinner," we advise the attorneys. We encourage the attorneys to put all five points on a single slide and show the entire story to jurors near the beginning of the opening statement. Then as the opening proceeds, we systematically return to each point and illustrate it with several key bits of evidence. This approach not only mimics the way jurors naïvely organize the case facts, but it also helps jurors to remember the evidence. The five points serve as mental file folders, where bits of evidence can be sorted and stored for quick retrieval later during deliberations. The narrative opening statement ideally takes no more than forty-five minutes to present.

The following are two examples of a five-point narrative opening statement in a generic auto-defect-allegation trial, as both the plaintiff and the defendant might tell the story.

Plaintiff's Story

1. Ms. X was killed and her daughter was seriously injured when their vehicle rolled over on the highway during a normal driving maneuver.
2. The rollover happened because the vehicle was unstable due to a design defect.
3. The manufacturer failed to test the vehicle adequately and tried to cover up the defect.
4. Even worse, the manufacturer never warned people about the defect, so drivers were unable to protect themselves and their families.
5. Because the manufacturer made and sold a vehicle with known design defects, improper testing, and inadequate warnings, which caused the accident that killed Ms. X and paralyzed her daughter, the manufacturer should face its responsibility, compensate the family for their losses, and be punished for its negligence.

This set of themes tells a satisfying story with a beginning, middle, and end. It lays out the entire plaintiff's case. And it organizes the evidence in a way that makes sense. In contrast, the defendant's themes would be something like the following.

Defendant's Story

1. Ms. X's accident happened because she accidentally drove off the road at a high speed, jerked the wheel to get back on the highway, and began sliding sideways down the road until her vehicle rolled over several times.
2. The vehicle was safe and stable and met all government standards for handling and stability.
3. Numerous tests showed that the vehicle remained upright during fore-seeable driving maneuvers, and there is no evidence that the vehicle was improperly tested.
4. The manufacturer clearly warned people that the vehicle required special handling and that drivers should not make extreme steering maneuvers at high speeds.
5. Because the manufacturer made a safe and stable vehicle, tested the vehicle thoroughly, and warned people about extreme steering maneuvers, it is unfair to blame the manufacturer for Ms. X's death and her daughter's injuries and to demand millions of dollars in compensatory and punitive damages.

Like the plaintiff's themes, this set of five themes also tells a satisfying story with a beginning, middle, and end. It organizes the defendant's evidence in a coherent way. And it tells why the defendant should not be blamed for the plaintiff's accident and injuries.

Having read each of the stories, you may find yourself already leaning toward one side or the other, even with such a generic set of facts. Which side you favor probably depends on how much you worry about risk, how suspicious you are of auto manufacturers, whether you have had similar experiences on the highway, and how much you identify with the plaintiff, among many other relevant attitudes and experiences that define you.

Connect Witnesses with the Case Story

After laying out the story of a case in the opening statement, it's important to link each of the witnesses back to the story. Often witnesses appear out of order, when it's convenient for them to fly in for the trial. Or the most credible witness is presented first, in the belief that the witness will make everything else seem more convincing. But each witness should be presented in story order, and each witness should be prepared to explain how his or her testimony fits into the overall story. Then jurors will better understand the importance of the witness' testimony.

Use the Closing Arguments to Tell the Story One Final Time
The closing arguments come at the very end of a trial, when the evidence has been presented and the attorneys have one last opportunity to pull the case together. But as I have already shown, the end of a trial is too late to pull anything together. Most jurors' minds have long been made up by then. Attorneys also like to play "gotcha" in their closing arguments. They accuse the other side of misrepresenting the evidence, of failing to respond to a point made by the opposing side, or of resorting to emotional appeals. While this may make for dramatic rhetoric, it is not the most effective way to handle the closing arguments. A much better use of the closing arguments is to review each of the themes from the opening statement and to remind jurors how the evidence confirmed the themes. This approach solidifies the jurors' grasp on the narrative and increases their confidence as they enter deliberations.

Develop Mentoring Programs for Young Attorneys
Because young attorneys have so few opportunities to present material to a jury, law firms need to help young attorneys gain trial experience. Instead of assigning less-experienced attorneys a minor role handling an obscure motion or using them to question low-level witnesses, law firms could allow young attorneys to assist in every phase of trial preparation and jury presentations. Shadowing a senior trial attorney would constitute true mentoring.[23]

Allow Jurors to Take Notes and Ask Questions
Imagine being required to sit through an upper-level college class that meets all day, Monday through Friday, for six to eight weeks, on a topic you know nothing about, such as the chemistry of diet drugs or the design of an electronic cruise-control device or the patent for a laser-surgery machine or the accuracy of an auditor's report. Now imagine that there will be no textbooks and you must rely entirely on spoken material delivered through lectures and interviews of experts and other witnesses. Finally, imagine being told that you cannot take notes or ask any questions of the presenters. You simply have to remember everything you heard without talking about it to anyone else, until you sit down with a group of strangers to assess what you were told. And hundreds of millions of dollars in damages may depend on what you decide. You have just imagined a high-stakes civil jury trial. Does any of it make any sense to you?

Allowing jurors to take notes during a trial is one of the most widely recommended reforms of the jury trial in America.[24] Nancy Marder, for example, concedes that taking notes might cause a juror to miss something important on the stand or to veer into doodling when a juror is bored or to rely on his or her notes during deliberations instead of reviewing key exhibits. But Marder stresses that note taking can focus a juror's attention on the presentations, help a juror to organize evidence as the trial progresses, and assist a juror's memory during deliberations.[25] Despite these obvious benefits, only a tiny percentage of judges allow jurors to take notes during a trial. Encouraging note taking would be a simple innovation that could have an enormous impact on jurors' verdicts.

As for allowing jurors to ask questions, Marder notes that a few judges are beginning to experiment with accepting written questions from jurors during a trial.[26] In a high-tech courtroom, where jurors enjoy individual computer workstations, the questions could be submitted electronically. The judge then decides if the question is permissible and advises the attorneys accordingly. While this may seem eminently reasonable, many judges and attorneys don't like the idea of accepting questions from the jurors. It weakens the judge's control over the courtroom and the attorneys' control over trial presentations. It may force an attorney to present information that was intentionally excluded. And it could empower a juror to become an advocate instead of a listener. However, the judge can always screen jurors' questions in advance and disallow advocacy questions. And allowing questions has the obvious benefits of reducing confusion, clarifying information, and removing speculation. It also makes sense.

Allow Predeliberation Discussion of Evidence

In nearly all federal and state courts, jurors are strictly admonished not to discuss the trial among themselves until they retire to deliberate. The notion is that jurors should not try to influence each other to reach a decision until all the evidence is in. But it is human nature for a group of people who spend days or weeks together to talk about what they are experiencing. In our own mock trials, we always instruct the jurors not to discuss the case during breaks, lunches, or on their ways in and out of the conference room. But we inevitably overhear jurors debating the case; lamenting the lack of certain information; and even commenting on the attorneys' skills, style, and dress.

While allowing predeliberation discussion of a case violates the tenet that jurors should not make up their minds until they retire to deliberate, it faces the fact that jurors will do this regardless of the judge's instruction. Marder notes that some judges believe such discussion is a "way for jurors to begin to process, organize and retain the wealth of information that is presented to them during the trial."[27] Other researchers say that predeliberation discussion increases jurors' comprehension of the case.[28] I agree with this and endorse the proposal that allowing predeliberation discussion would be not only realistic because jurors will do it anyway but also beneficial as a means of helping jurors process the trial information.

How Can We Make Jury Deliberations More Effective?

Although little is known about how jurors behave during actual trial deliberations, my own post-trial interviews with hundreds of jurors and my experience observing mock juries shows that jurors' performance during deliberations runs the gamut. Some people clam up and say almost nothing; others try to take over and run the show. Some barely understand the evidence; others think they understood it but manage to ignore whatever evidence fails to fit their theories. Occasionally, the group enters the jury room with a unanimous or near-unanimous decision; other times, the group is split down the middle.

If jurors discover they all agree at the outset, then they typically skim over the evidence and declare a verdict. If a consensus gradually forms, then the jurors in the majority often hammer the minority jurors to justify their positions or give up. If the minority jurors refuse to cave in, either because of the strength of their beliefs or because there is no face-saving way to change their minds, then the majority tends to ignore them. Sometimes a minority juror will finally acquiesce in response to group pressure or for the sake of harmony. Occasionally, a juror will frankly admit that he or she just wants to go home and doesn't care what the group decides. Seldom does a jury dispassionately analyze each piece of evidence, weigh the pros and cons, and reason out a verdict.

As mentioned earlier, decision-making groups often suffer from groupthink. The more isolated a group is, the more important it is, the more stress it feels, and the more it is expected to reach a consensus, the more likely it is to suffer groupthink. Under groupthink, the group members are so driven to seek consensus and reach a unanimous decision that they fail to appraise alternative courses of action and sometimes make mistakes. In the words of psychologist Irving Janis, who first wrote about groupthink, they can suffer a "deterioration of mental efficiency, reality testing, and moral judgment that results from in-group pressures." Put more simply, "they rush to judgment."[29]

Instruct Juries on How to Conduct Deliberations and Avoid Groupthink

Because juries are highly susceptible to groupthink, jurors should be informed about strategies to help avoid the mistakes of groupthink. One of the leading researchers in jury decision making, Reid Hastie, has teamed up with a lead-ing behavioral economist, Cass Sunstein, to write a book about how groups can make smarter decisions.[30] Other researchers have also proposed tech-niques for juries to avoid groupthink.[31] Their combined suggestions include the following:

- Allow all jurors to state a position before any juror begins advocat-ing for a position. Jurors typically begin deliberations by allowing or encouraging each person to reveal his or her stance on a likely verdict before they have discussed the evidence. Sometimes, two or three dif-ferent "stories" emerge at the outset, and alliances begin to form. Other times, a dominant juror or two may begin contesting another juror's story. It is important at this point to hear all the stories before arguing why one story is better than another.
- Ask jurors to state the evidence that led to their decisions. Jurors often cite a single highly convincing piece of evidence as the reason for their verdict. Or they use a commonsense rationale to explain their decision. Very seldom will a juror be able to cite three or four bits of evidence that were most convincing and at the same time explain why other evidence was not convincing. To counter this tendency, each juror should be asked to cite the pros and cons of evidence that mattered in his or her decision making, a task that would be assisted by note taking during the trial.
- Encourage minority viewpoints. Before consensus builds too quickly, the foreperson and other jurors should seek out the position of jurors in the minority. Ask them to explain their positions without leaping to refute or attack. Inquire whether other jurors can see some truth in the minority views.
- As consensus builds, ask jurors to criticize their own or others' positions. The most common recipe for resisting groupthink is asking members of the majority to play devil's advocate for the minority, or rejected, posi-tion. What's the weakest evidence for the majority position? What could go wrong if we decide in favor of that position? What unforeseen consequences might there be? Likewise, individual jurors can be asked to state what they view as the weakest reason for their decision.
- Allow a face-saving rationale for jurors who change their minds. Instead of ignoring or badgering jurors who seem to be holdouts, the foreperson and other vocal jurors should offer them an avenue for change: "Now that you heard this other perspective on the evidence you relied on, how does that affect your conclusions?" Or "How certain are you about

your position, in light of what the others have said?" Some jurors will sincerely change their minds. Others will use the offered hand as a cover for simply acquiescing without actually changing their minds.

- Call for a last-chance discussion before reaching a final verdict: "Is everyone comfortable with this decision? What's the chance of this being the wrong decision? Could anything make us change our minds?" In order to help juries to avoid groupthink, the judge could provide the jurors with a written set of suggestions about how to deliberate. Most jurors would welcome such guidance. The resulting deliberations would be much richer and more careful than if jurors were left to their own devices.

Restoring the Jury

This chapter begins with the claim, in some quarters, that the jury system is broken and can't be fixed. But this book advances many proposals for reforming the jury system and restoring trial by jury as a trusted source of justice. Altogether, these proposals include the following:

- Broaden the base for obtaining potential jurors' names.
- Require more people to respond to a jury summons.
- Grant fewer excuses for jury duty.
- Encourage judges to manage disputes toward expeditious jury trials and not toward settlement.
- Ask jurors to fill out written questionnaires before they appear for jury selection.
- Allow fewer peremptory strikes to remove potential jurors from a jury.
- Simplify the judge's instructions and move them to the beginning of a trial.
- Teach attorneys how to present narrative opening statements that tell a story with a beginning, middle, and end.
- Connect witnesses with the case story.
- Use the closing arguments to tell the story one final time.
- Develop mentoring programs for young attorneys.
- Allow jurors to take notes and ask questions.
- Allow predeliberation discussion of evidence.
- Instruct juries on how to conduct deliberations and avoid groupthink:
  o Allow all jurors to state a position before any juror begins advocating for a position.
  o Ask jurors to state the evidence that led to their decisions.
  o Encourage minority viewpoints.

o As consensus builds, ask jurors to play devil's advocate for their own or others' positions.

o Allow a face-saving rationale for jurors who change their minds.

o Call for a last-chance discussion before reaching a final verdict.

With changes like these, we would be more likely to avoid such trial outcomes as the Dewey & LeBoeuf case in the introduction to this book. In that case, jurors sat through a four-and-a-half-month trial, deliberated for twenty-one days, and then informed the judge that they were hopelessly deadlocked. A federal district court judge who followed the case has this advice about how to avoid such trial outcomes: "Keep it simple. A jury that understands the basics can reason through to a verdict. A jury that's confused is a recipe for bizarre results. If the charge is simple and the presentation is straightforward, then the issues become relatively clear cut."[32] A psychologist who was asked to comment on the Dewey & LeBoeuf jurors explains, "They're hungering for a story to tie together all these disparate facts. Trials are like movies. There's a plot, and if the plot doesn't make sense, jurors get confused."[33]

Summary

This book approaches trial by jury from the perspective of cognitive social psychology. I have reviewed how and why people construct stories in order to make sense of trial evidence: because the human brain evolved to favor System 1 narrative thinking over System 2 rational analysis. For hundreds of years, this kind of quick, narrative decision making was how juries operated. As trials have become longer and more complex, quick, narrative decision making has led most jurors to lean toward one side or the other very early in the trial, often during the opening statements. Jurors then return to this early leaning at the end of the trial, when they declare their verdicts.

Jury trials are so disparaged for their cost, length, and seemingly reckless verdicts that trial by jury is on the road to extinction. But doing away with juries in favor of experts—that is, judges, mediators, and arbitrators—offers no solution to the just verdict problem. Experts resort to storytelling and cognitive shortcuts, just as jurors do. And experts' decisions are not filtered through the countervailing biases of a jury of one's peers.

The real solution for obtaining clearer, more reasonable verdicts that are more reflective of a cross-section of communities is to respect the brain's capacities—that is, to present trial evidence in a more narrative format. Likewise, judges' instructions should be written in street language, and they should be presented at the very beginning of a trial, so jurors understand their tasks. Citizens, better educated and more motivated, must also do their part by agreeing to become jurors and taking the job seriously.

With such reforms as these, ordinary people who represent diverse interests can still reason together toward just verdicts. Juries' decisions can still maintain the foundation of a democratic moral culture. The bottom line on trial by jury is that juries need not vanish; they should be nurtured.

Notes

Introduction

1. Matthew Goldstein, "Mistrial Is Declared in Dewey & LeBouef Case," *New York Times*, October 19, 2015; James B. Stewart, "Dewey Jury's Deadlock Exposes a System's Flaws," *New York Times*, November 5, 2015.

2. Graham Bowley, Richard Perez-Pena, and Jon Hurdle, "Bill Cosby's Sexual Assault Case Ends in a Mistrial," *New York Times*, June 17, 2017.

3. Lawrence Crook III, Walter Imparato, and Eric Levenson, "Bill Cosby Juror Speaks: 'We Had No Real New Evidence,'" *CNN*, June 23, 2017, https://www.cnn.com/2017/06/23/us/bill-cosby-juror-speak/index.html.

4. Adam Benforado, *Unfair: The New Science of Criminal Justice* (New York: Crown, 2015); Adam Benforado, "Flawed Humans, Flawed Justice," *New York Times*, June 13, 2015; Adam Benforado, "Reasonable Doubts about the Jury System," *Atlantic*, June 6, 2015.

Chapter Two

1. Frederick Pollock and Frederic Maitland, *The History of English Common Law before the Time of Edward I* (Cambridge: Cambridge University Press, 1898), 138.

2. Dennis Hale, *The Jury in America: Triumph and Decline* (Lawrence, KS: University of Kansas Press, 2016), 7.

3. Thomas. A. Green, *Verdict According to Conscience: Perspectives on the English Criminal Trial Jury, 1200–1800* (Chicago: University of Chicago Press, 1985), 16.

4. Ibid.

5. Neil Vidmar and Valerie Hans, *American Juries: The Verdict* (Amherst, NY: Prometheus Books, 2007), 24.

6. Green, *Verdict According to Conscience*, 68n7.

7. Hale, *Jury in America*, 11.

8. Daniel Klerman, "Was the Jury Ever Self-Informing?" *Southern California Law Review* 77, no. 1 (2003): 123–50.

9. David J. Seipp, "Jurors, Evidences, and the Tempest of 1499," in *The Dearest Birth Right of the People of England: The Jury in the History of Common Law*, ed. John W. Cairns and Grant McLeod (Oxford: Hart, 2002), 82–85; John H. Langbein, Renee L. Lerner, and Bruce P. Smith, *History of the Common Law: The Development of Anglo-American Legal Institutions* (Austin, TX: Wolters Kluwer, 2009), 240.

10. Green, *Verdict According to Conscience*, 43.

11. Langbein, Lerner, and Smith, *History of the Common Law*, 244.

12. Hale, *Jury in America*, 18.

13. Vidmar and Hans, *American Juries*, 47.

14. Ibid., 42.

15. Seipp, "Jurors, Evidences," 85.

16. Alexander Pope, "The Rape of the Lock," in *Alexander Pope: The Major Works* (Oxford: Oxford University Press, 2009; first published in 1717).

17. Vidmar and Hans, *American Juries*, 35.

18. Ibid., 60.

19. Lawrence M. Friedman, "The Day before Trials Vanished," *Journal of Empirical Legal Studies* 1, no. 3, (November 2004): 689–703.

20. D. Graham Burnett, *Trying Leviathan: The Nineteenth-Century Court Case That Put the Whale on Trial and Challenged the Order of Nature* (Princeton, NJ: Princeton University Press, 2007).

21. Ibid., 191.

Chapter Three

1. Nancy Pennington and Reid Hastie, "The Story Model for Jury Decision Making," in *Inside the Juror*, ed. Reid Hastie (Cambridge: Cambridge University Press, 1993), 192–222.

2. Nancy Pennington and Reid Hastie, "Explaining the Evidence: Tests of the Story Model for Jury Decision Making," *Journal of Personality and Social Psychology* 62, no. 2 (1992): 189–206.

3. Ibid., 193–95.

4. Pennington and Hastie, "Story Model," 192–222.

Chapter Four

1. Daniel Kahneman, *Thinking, Fast and Slow* (New York: Farrar, Strauss, and Giroux, 2011).

2. Ibid., 87.

3. Daniel A. Krauss, John G. McCabe, and Joel D. Lieberman, "Dangerously Misunderstood: Representative Juror's Reactions to Expert Testimony on Future

Dangerousness in a Sexually Violent Predator Trial," *Psychology, Public Policy, and Law* 18, no. 1 (February 2012): 18–49, doi:1037/a0024550.

4. Joel D. Lieberman, Daniel A. Krauss, Mariel Kyger, and Maribeth Lehoux, "Determining Dangerousness in Sexually Violent Predator Evaluations: Cognitive-Experiential Self-Theory and Juror Judgments of Expert Testimony," *Behavioral Sciences and the Law* 25, no. 4 (July–August 2007), doi:10.1002/bsl.771.

5. Kahneman, *Thinking, Fast and Slow*, 417.

6. Dennis J. Devine, *Jury Decision Making: The State of the Science* (New York: New York University Press, 2012), 193–94.

7. Harry Kalven Jr. and Hans Zeisel, *The American Jury* (Boston: Little, Brown, 1966).

8. Hans Zeisel, "A Jury Hoax: The Superpower of the Opening Statement," *Litigation* 14, no. 4 (Summer 1988): 17–18.

Chapter Five

1. Rachel Delinsky, "Jury Deliberation Begins," *Sanford Herald*, July 12, 2013.

2. Ibid.

3. Reid Hastie, Steven Penrod, and Nancy Pennington, *Inside the Jury* (Cambridge, MA: Harvard University Press, 1983).

4. Andrew Branca, "Zimmerman Jury Selection: Day Eight Wrap-Up," *Legal Insurrection*, June 19, 2013, https://legalinsurrection.com/2013/06/zimmerman-jury-selection-day-eight-wrap-up.

5. Shamena Anwar, Patrick Bayer, and Randi Hjalmarsson, "The Impact of Jury Race in Criminal Trials," *Quarterly Journal of Economics* 127, no. 2 (May 1, 2012): 1017–55, doi:10.1093/qje/qjs014.

6. David Ovalle and Audra D. S. Burch, "Jury Seated in Zimmerman Trial," *Miami Herald*, June 20, 2013.

7. Yamiche Alcindor, "Zimmerman Consultant Wanted All Female Jury," *USA Today*, July 18, 2013.

8. Dana Ford, "George Zimmerman Was 'Justified' in Shooting Trayvon Martin, Juror Says," *CNN*, July 17, 2013, https://www.cnn.com/2013/07/16/us/zimmerman-juror/index.html.

9. Lizette Alvarez, "Juror Says Zimmerman 'Got Away with Murder,'" *New York Times*, July 26, 2013, 11.

10. Delinsky, "Jury Deliberation Begins."

Chapter Six

1. Sean Overland, *The Juror Factor: Race and Gender in America's Civil Courts* (El Paso, TX: LFB Scholarly, 2009).

2. Ibid., 79.

3. Dana Ford, "George Zimmerman Was 'Justified' in Shooting Trayvon Martin, Juror Says," *CNN*, July 17, 2013, https://www.cnn.com/2013/07/16/us/zimmerman-juror/index.html.

Chapter Seven

1. Dennis J. Devine, *Jury Decision Making: The State of the Science* (New York: New York University Press, 2012).
2. Irving L. Janis, *Victims of Groupthink* (Boston: Houghton Mifflin, 1972).
3. David H. Mitchell and Daniel Eckstein, "Jury Dynamics and Decision Making: A Prescription for Groupthink," *International Journal of Academic Research* 1, no. 1 (September 2009).
4. Devine, *Jury Decision Making*, 43–44.
5. Ibid., 154.
6. Ibid., 159.
7. Harry Kalven Jr. and Hans Zeisel, *The American Jury* (New York: Little, Brown, 1966).
8. Devine, *Jury Decision Making*, 159.
9. Robert J. K. MacCoun, "Experimental Research on Jury Decision Making," *Science* 244 (June 2, 1989): 1046–50.

Chapter Nine

1. C. K. Rowland, Tina Traficanti, and Erin Vernon, "Every Jury Trial Is a Bench Trial: Judicial Engineering of Jury Disputes," in *The Psychology of Judicial Decision Making*, ed. David Klein and Gregory Mitchell (Oxford: Oxford University Press, 2010), 183–201.

Chapter Ten

1. Lee Epstein, William M. Landis, and Richard A. Posner, *The Behavior of Federal Judges* (Cambridge, MA: Harvard University Press, 2013).
2. Ibid., 309.
3. Cass R. Sunstein, David Schkade, and Lisa Michelle Ellman, "Ideological Voting on Federal Courts of Appeals: A Preliminary Investigation," *Virginia Law Review* 90, no. 1 (March 2004): 301–54.
4. Ibid.
5. Alma Cohen and Crystal Yang, "Judicial Politics and Sentencing Decisions" (NBER Working Paper No. w24615, May 2018), https://ssrn.com/abstract=3182214.
6. Epstein, Landis, and Posner, *Behavior of Federal Judges*.
7. Gregory Sisk, Michael Heise, and Andrew Morris, "Charting the Influences on the Judicial Mind: An Empirical Study of Judicial Reasoning," *New York Law Review* 73, no. 5 (November 1998): 1377–500.

8. Epstein, Landis, and Posner, *Behavior of Federal Judges*, 385.

9. Chris Guthrie, Jeffrey Rachlinski, and Andrew Wistrich, "Inside the Judicial Mind," *Cornell Law Review* 86, no. 4 (May 2001): 780.

10. Ibid., 791.

11. Ibid., 788.

12. Daniel Kahneman, *Thinking, Fast and Slow* (New York: Farrar, Strauss, and Giroux, 2011), 125–26.

13. Guthrie, Rachlinski, and Wistrich, "Inside the Judicial Mind," 791.

14. Kahneman, *Thinking, Fast and Slow*, 201–4.

15. Guthrie, Rachlinski, and Wistrich, "Inside the Judicial Mind," 801–3.

16. Ibid., 779.

17. Holgar Spamann and Lars Klohn, "Justice Is Less Blind, and Less Legalistic, Than We Thought: Evidence from an Experiment with Real Judges," *Journal of Legal Studies* 49 (June 2016).

18. Dennis J. Devine, *Jury Decision Making: The State of the Science* (New York: New York University Press, 2012), 14–15.

19. Niel Vidmar and Valerie Hans, *American Juries: The Verdict* (Amherst, NY: Prometheus Books, 2007), 148–51.

20. Ibid., 150–51.

Chapter Eleven

1. Marc Galanter, "A World without Trials," *Journal of Dispute Resolution* 7 (2006): 21–26.

2. Stephen D. Susman, "Disappearing Civil Trials" (paper presented at the 35th Annual Conference of American Society of Trial Consultants, May 20, 2016).

3. Robert P. Burns, *The Death of the American Trial* (Chicago: University of Chicago Press, 2009).

4. Marc Galanter and Angela Frozena, "The Continuing Decline of Civil Trials in American Courts" (paper presented at the Forum for State Appellate Court Judges, Pound Civil Institute, 2011); Joe Palazzolo, "Courtroom Surprise: Fewer Tort Lawsuits," *Wall Street Journal*, July 25, 2017.

5. Mark Curriden, "Number of Jury Trials Declines to New Lows in Texas," *Dallas Morning News*, June 22, 2013.

6. Galanter and Frozena, "Continuing Decline."

7. Lawrence M. Friedman, "The Day before Trials Vanished," *Journal of Empirical Legal Studies* 1, no. 3 (November 2004): 689–703.

8. Quoted in Benjamin Weiser, "Trial by Jury, a Hallowed American Right, Is Vanishing," *New York Times*, August 7, 2016.

9. Galanter, "World without Trials," 21–26.

10. Marc Galanter, "The Vanishing Trial: An Examination of Trials and Related Matters in Federal and State Courts," *Journal of Empirical Legal Studies* 1, no. 3 (November 2004): 459–570.

11. Friedman, "Day before Trials Vanished."

12. Ibid., 689.

13. John H. Langbein, "The Disappearance of Civil Trial in the United States," *Yale Law Journal* 122 (2012): 522.

14. Ibid., 551.

15. Galanter, "Vanishing Trial."

16. Langbein, "Disappearance of Civil Trial," 560.

17. Galanter, "Vanishing Trial."

18. Galanter, "World without Trials," 21–26.

19. Sheldon Whitehouse, "Restoring the Civil Jury's Role in the Structure of Our Government," *William and Mary Law Review* 55, no. 3 (2014).

20. Jessica Silver-Greenberg and Robert Gebeloff, "Arbitration Everywhere: Stacking the Deck of Justice," *New York Times*, November 1, 2015, 1.

Chapter Twelve

1. Mark Curriden, "Number of Jury Trials Declines to New Lows in Texas," *Dallas Morning News*, June 22, 2013, 6.

2. Marc Galanter, "A World without Trials," *Journal of Dispute Resolution* 7 (2006): 21–26.

3. Ibid., 7.

4. Stephen D. Susman, "Disappearing Civil Trials" (paper presented at the 35th Annual Conference of American Society of Trial Consultants, May 20, 2016), 16.

5. David R. Fine, Lucille A. Marsh, and Thomas B. Schmidt III, "The 'Vanishing' Civil Jury Trial," *Voir Dire* (Spring 2010).

6. Randall T. Shepard, "State Court Reform of the American Jury," *Yale Law Journal, Pocket* 117 (2008).

7. Philip E. Tetlock, *Expert Political Judgment: How Good Is It? How Can We Know?* (Princeton, NJ: Princeton University Press, 2005).

8. Daniel Kahneman, *Thinking, Fast and Slow* (New York: Farrar, Straus, and Giroux, 2011), 417.

9. Ibid., 417–18.

10. Sheldon Whitehouse, "Restoring the Civil Jury's Role in the Structure of Our Government," *William and Mary Law Review* 55, no. 3 (2014): 1272.

11. Robert P. Burns, *The Death of the American Trial* (Chicago: University of Chicago Press, 2009).

12. Nancy S. Marder, "Introduction to the Jury at a Crossroad: The American Experience," *Chicago-Kent Law Review* 78, no. 3, (2003): 922.

13. Burns, *Death of the American Trial*, 113.

14. D. Graham Burnett, *A Trial by Jury* (New York: Vintage Books 2001).

15. Ibid., 73–74.

16. Ibid., 137.

17. Stephan Landsman, "Appellate Courts and Civil Juries," *University of Cincinnati Law Review* 70 (2002): 873–911.

18. Marder, "Introduction to the Jury," 922.

Chapter Thirteen

1. Jeffrey Abramson, *We the Jury: The Jury System and the Ideal of Democracy* (New York: Basic Books, 1994).

2. Ibid.

3. Ibid.

4. Ibid., 123.

5. Ibid.

6. Nancy Marder, *The Jury Process* (New York: Foundation Press, 2005).

7. Neil Vidmar and Valerie Hans, *American Juries: The Verdict* (Amherst, NY: Prometheus Books, 2005).

8. Valerie Hans and Stephanie Albertson, "Empirical Research and Civil Jury Reform" (Cornell Law Faculty Publications, Paper 310, 2003).

9. Rebecca Love Kourlis and Gilbert A. Dickenson, "Why the Disappearance of Civil Trials Is Not Acceptable," *Voir Dire* (Fall/Winter 2010): 5–8.

10. Robert P. Burns, *The Death of the American Trial* (Chicago: University of Chicago Press, 2009).

11. J. A. Simpson and E. S. C. Weiner, eds., *The Oxford English Dictionary*, 2nd ed. (Oxford: Clarendon Press, 1989).

12. Ibid.; Dennis J. Divine, *Jury Decision Making: The State of the Science* (New York: New York University Press, 2012); Akhil Reed Amar, "Reinventing Juries: Ten Suggested Reforms" (Faculty Scholarship Series, Paper 988, Yale Law School, 1995).

13. Divine, *Jury Decision Making*, 57–58.

14. Abramson, *We the Jury*, 91.

15. Divine, *Jury Decision Making*, 229.

16. Ibid.

17. Burns, *Death of the American Trial*, 113–16; Divine, *Jury Decision Making*, 193–201; Vidmar and Hans, *American Juries*, 343–44.

18. Divine, *Jury Decision Making*, 193–201, 228.

19. Vidmar and Hans, *American Juries*, 343–44.

20. Yvette Tinsley, "Juror Decision-Making: A Look inside the Juror Room," *British Society of Criminology: Selected Proceedings* 4 (October 2001): 4.

21. Burns, *Death of the American Trial*, 114.

22. George A. Miller, "The Magic Number Seven Plus or Minus Two: Some Limits on Our Ability for Processing Information," *Psychological Review* 63, no. 2 (1956): 81–97.

23. David R. Fine, Lucille A. Marsh, and Thomas B. Schmidt III, "The 'Vanishing' Civil Jury Trial," *Voir Dire* (Spring 2010).

24. Hans and Albertson, "Empirical Research," 1511; Vidmar and Hans, *American Juries*; Divine, *Jury Decision Making*.

25. Marder, *Jury Process*.

26. Ibid.

27. Ibid., 115.

28. Hans and Albertson, "Empirical Research."

29. Irving L. Janis, *Groupthink*, 2nd ed. (Boston: Houghton Mifflin, 1983), 9.

30. Cass R. Sunstein and Reid Hastie, *Wiser: Getting beyond Groupthink to Make Groups Smarter* (Boston: Harvard Business Review Press, 2015).

31. David H. Mitchell and Daniel Eckstein, "Jury Dynamics and Decision Making: A Prescription for Groupthink," *International Journal of Academic Research* 1, no. 1 (September 2009).

32. James B. Stewart, "Dewey Jury's Deadlock Exposes a System's Flaws," *New York Times*, November 5, 2015.

33. Ibid.

Bibliography

Abramson, Jeffrey. *We the Jury: The Jury System and the Ideal of Democracy.* New York: Basic Books, 1994.

Alcindor, Yamiche. "Zimmerman Consultant Wanted All Female Jury." *USA Today,* July 18, 2013.

Alvarez, Lizette. "Juror Says Zimmerman 'Got Away with Murder.'" *New York Times,* July 26, 2013.

Amar, Akhil Reed. "Reinventing Juries: Ten Suggested Reforms." Faculty Scholarship Series, Paper 988, Yale Law School, 1995.

Anwar, Shamena, Patrick Bayer, and Randi Hjalmarsson. "The Impact of Jury Race in Criminal Trials." *Quarterly Journal of Economics* 127, no. 2 (May 1, 2012): 1017–155. doi:10.1093/qje/qjs014.

Benforado, Adam. "Flawed Humans, Flawed Justice." *New York Times,* June 13, 2015.

———. "Reasonable Doubts about the Jury System." *Atlantic,* June 6, 2015.

———. *Unfair: The New Science of Criminal Justice.* New York: Crown, 2015.

Bowley, Graham, Richard Perez-Pena, and Jon Hurdle. "Bill Cosby's Sexual Assault Case Ends in a Mistrial." *New York Times,* June 17, 2017.

Branca, Andrew. "Zimmerman Jury Selection: Day Eight Wrap-Up." *Legal Insurrection.* June 19, 2013. https://legalinsurrection.com/2013/06/zimmerman-jury-selection-day-eight-wrap-up.

Burnett, D. Graham. *A Trial by Jury.* New York: Vintage Books, 2001.

———. *Trying Leviathan: The Nineteenth-Century Court Case That Put the Whale on Trial and Challenged the Order of Nature.* Princeton, NJ: Princeton University Press, 2007.

Burns, Robert P. *The Death of the American Trial.* Chicago: University of Chicago Press, 2009.

Cohen, Alma, and Crystal Yang. "Judicial Politics and Sentencing Decisions." NBER Working Paper No. w24615, May 2018. https://ssrn.com/abstract=3182214.

Crook, Lawrence, III, Walter Imparato, and Eric Levenson, "Bill Cosby Juror Speaks: 'We Had No Real New Evidence.'" *CNN.* June 23, 2017. https://www.cnn.com/2017/06/23/us/bill-cosby-juror-speak/index.html.

Curriden Mark. "Number of Jury Trials Declines to New Lows in Texas." *Dallas Morning News,* June 22, 2013.

Delinsky, Rachel. "Jury Deliberation Begins." *Sanford Herald,* July 12, 2013.

Devine, Dennis J. *Jury Decision Making: The State of the Science.* New York: New York University Press, 2012.

Epstein, Lee, William M. Landis, and Richard A. Posner. *The Behavior of Federal Judges.* Cambridge, MA: Harvard University Press, 2013.

Fine, David R., Lucille A. Marsh, and Thomas B. Schmidt III. "The 'Vanishing' Civil Jury Trial." *Voir Dire* (Spring 2010).

Ford, Dana. "George Zimmerman Was 'Justified' in Shooting Trayvon Martin, Juror Says." *CNN.* July 17, 2013. https://www.cnn.com/2013/07/16/us/zimmerman-juror/index.html.

Friedman, Lawrence M. "The Day before Trials Vanished." *Journal of Empirical Legal Studies* 1, no. 3 (November 2004): 689–703.

Galanter, Marc. "The Vanishing Trial: An Examination of Trials and Related Matters in Federal and State Courts." *Journal of Empirical Legal Studies* 1, no. 3 (November 2004): 459–570.

———. "A World without Trials." *Journal of Dispute Resolution* 7 (2006): 21–26.

Galanter, Marc, and Angela Frozena. "The Continuing Decline of Civil Trials in American Courts." Paper presented at the Forum for State Appellate Court Judges, Pound Civil Institute, 2011.

Goldstein, Matthew. "Mistrial Is Declared in Dewey & LeBouef Case." *New York Times,* October 19, 2015.

Green, Thomas A. *Verdict According to Conscience: Perspectives on the English Criminal Trial Jury, 1200–1800.* Chicago: University of Chicago Press, 1985.

Guthrie, Chris, Jeffrey Rachlinski, and Andrew Wistrich. "Inside the Judicial Mind." *Cornell Law Review* 86, no. 4 (May 2001): 777–830.

Hale, Dennis. *The Jury in America: Triumph and Decline.* Lawrence: University of Kansas Press, 2016.

Hans, Valerie, and Stephanie Albertson. "Empirical Research and Civil Jury Reform." Cornell Law Faculty Publications, Paper 310, 2003.

Hastie, Reid, Steven Penrod, and Nancy Pennington. *Inside the Jury.* Cambridge, MA: Harvard University Press, 1983.

Janis, Irving L. *Groupthink.* 2nd ed. Boston: Houghton Mifflin, 1983.

———. *Victims of Groupthink.* Boston: Houghton Mifflin, 1972.

Kahneman, Daniel. *Thinking, Fast and Slow.* New York: Farrar, Strauss, and Giroux, 2011.

Kalven, Harry, Jr., and Hans Zeisel. *The American Jury.* Boston: Little, Brown, 1966.

Klerman, Daniel. "Was the Jury Ever Self-Informing?" *Southern California Law Review* 77, no. 1 (2003).

Kourlis, Rebecca Love, and Gilbert A. Dickenson. "Why the Disappearance of Civil Trials Is Not Acceptable." *Voir Dire* (Fall/Winter 2010): 5–8.

Krauss, Daniel A., John G. McCabe, and Joel D. Lieberman. "Dangerously Misunderstood: Representative Juror's Reactions to Expert Testimony on Future Dangerousness in a Sexually Violent Predator Trial." *Psychology, Public Policy, and Law* 18, no. 1 (February 2012): 18–49. doi:1037/a0024550.

Landsman, Stephan. "Appellate Courts and Civil Juries." *University of Cincinnati Law Review*, 70 (2002): 873–911.

Langbein, John H. "The Disappearance of Civil Trial in the United States." *Yale Law Journal* 122 (2012): 522–72.

Langbein, John H., Renee L. Lerner, and Bruce P. Smith. *History of the Common Law: The Development of Anglo-American Legal Institutions*. Austin, TX: Wolters Kluwer, 2009.

Lieberman, Joel D., Daniel A. Krauss, Mariel Kyger, and Maribeth Lehoux. "Determining Dangerousness in Sexually Violent Predator Evaluations: Cognitive-Experiential Self-Theory and Juror Judgments of Expert Testimony." *Behavioral Sciences and the Law* 25, no. 4 (July–August 2007). doi:10.1002/bsl.771.

MacCoun, Robert J. K. "Experimental Research on Jury Decision Making," *Science* 244 (June 2, 1989): 1046–50.

Marder, Nancy S. "Introduction to the Jury at a Crossroad: The American Experience." 78, no. 3 *Chicago-Kent Law Review* (2003): 909–33.

———. *The Jury Process*. New York: Foundation Press, 2005.

Miller, George A. "The Magic Number Seven Plus or Minus Two: Some Limits on Our Ability for Processing Information." *Psychological Review* 63, no. 2 (1956): 81–97.

Mitchell, David H., and Daniel Eckstein. "Jury Dynamics and Decision Making: A Prescription for Groupthink." *International Journal of Academic Research* 1, no. 1 (September 2009).

Ovalle, David, and Audra D. S. Burch. "Jury Seated in Zimmerman Trial." *Miami Herald*, June 20, 2013.

Overland, Sean. *The Juror Factor: Race and Gender in America's Civil Courts*. El Paso, TX: LFB Scholarly, 2009.

Palazzolo, Joe. "Courtroom Surprise: Fewer Tort Lawsuits." *Wall Street Journal*, July 25, 2017.

Pennington, Nancy, and Reid Hastie. "Explaining the Evidence: Tests of the Story Model for Jury Decision Making." *Journal of Personality and Social Psychology* 62, no. 2 (1992).

———. "The Story Model for Jury Decision Making." In *Inside the Juror*, edited by Reid Hastie, 192–222. Cambridge: Cambridge University Press, 1993.

Pollock, Frederick, and Frederic Maitland. *The History of English Common Law before the Time of Edward I*. Cambridge: Cambridge University Press, 1898.

Pope, Alexander. "The Rape of the Lock." In *Alexander Pope: The Major Works*. Oxford: Oxford University Press, 2009; first published in 1717.

Rowland, C. K., Tina Traficanti, and Erin Vernon. "Every Jury Trial Is a Bench Trial: Judicial Engineering of Jury Disputes." In *The Psychology of Judicial Decision Making*, edited by David Klein and Gregory Mitchell. Oxford: Oxford University Press, 2010.

Seipp, David J. "Jurors, Evidences, and the Tempest of 1499." In *The Dearest Birth Right of the People of England: The Jury in the History of Common Law*, edited by John W. Cairns and Grant McLeod, 75–92. Oxford: Hart, 2002.

Shepard, Randall, T. "State Court Reform of the American Jury." *Yale Law Journal* 117 (2008).

Silver-Greenberg, Jessica, and Robert Gebeloff. "Arbitration Everywhere: Stacking the Deck of Justice." *New York Times*, November 1, 2015.

Simpson, J. A., and E. S. C. Weiner, eds. *The Oxford English Dictionary*. 2nd ed. Oxford: Clarendon Press, 1989.

Sisk, Gregory, Michael Heise, and Andrew Morris. "Charting the Influences on the Judicial Mind: An Empirical Study of Judicial Reasoning." *New York Law Review* 73, no. 5 (November 1998): 1377–500.

Spamann, Holger, and Lars Klohn. "Justice Is Less Blind, and Less Legalistic, Than We Thought: Evidence from an Experiment with Real Judges." *Journal of Legal Studies* 49 (June 2016).

Stewart, James B. "Dewey Jury's Deadlock Exposes a System's Flaws." *New York Times*, November 5, 2015.

Sunstein, Cass R., David Schkade, and Lisa Michelle Ellman. "Ideological Voting on Federal Courts of Appeals: A Preliminary Investigation." *Virginia Law Review* 90, no. 1 (March 2004): 301–54.

Sunstein, Cass R., and Reid Hastie. *Wiser: Getting beyond Groupthink to Make Groups Smarter*. Boston: Harvard Business Review Press, 2015.

Susman, Stephen D. "Disappearing Civil Trials." Paper presented at the 35th Annual Conference of American Society of Trial Consultants, May 20, 2016.

Tetlock, Philip E. *Expert Political Judgment: How Good Is It? How Can We Know?* Princeton, NJ: Princeton University Press, 2005.

Tinsley, Yvette. "Juror Decision-Making: A Look inside the Juror Room." *British Society of Criminology: Selected Proceedings* 4 (October 2001).

Vidmar, Neil, and Valerie Hans. *American Juries: The Verdict*. Amherst, NY: Prometheus Books, 2007.

Weiser, Benjamin. "Trial by Jury, a Hallowed American Right, Is Vanishing." *New York Times*, August 7, 2016.

Whitehouse, Sheldon. "Restoring the Civil Jury's Role in the Structure of Our Government." *William and Mary Law Review* 55, no. 3 (2014).

Zeisel, Hans. "A Jury Hoax: The Superpower of the Opening Statement." *Litigation* 14, no. 4 (Summer 1988): 17–18.

Index

About the Author

Drury Sherrod, PhD, is the co-founder of Mattson & Sherrod, Inc. Sherrod is a member of the American Society of Trial Consultants, the American Psychological Association, and the Society for Experimental Social Psychology. Along with authoring *Social Psychology* (1982), he has authored more than thirty articles on psychology, jury behavior, attribution theory and the effects of environmental stress on human behavior. Sherrod has given many talks on jury trials and juries in America to a variety of audiences, including college classes, law firms, bar associations, legal conferences, professional associations and groups interested in law and the social sciences, and has also presented research findings to hundreds of attorneys in law firms across the United States.